MARCO 🌐 POLO

GW00643889

NCH
RIV
IERA

NICE CANNES MONACO

BELGIUM

LUX.

Rhine

GER-
MANY

Paris

Seine

Loire

Dijon

SWITZERLAND

FRANCE

Lyon

ITALY

Bordeaux

Rhône

Marseille

Nice

MO.

AND.

French Riviera
*Mediterranean
Sea*

FREE!

THE
TOURING APP

shows you the way...
including routes and offline maps!

GET MORE OUT OF YOUR MARCO POLO GUIDE

IT'S AS SIMPLE AS THIS

1 go.marco-polo.com/frr

2 download and discover

GO!

WORKS OFFLINE!

SYMBOLS

INSIDER TIP	Insider Tip
★	Highlight
●●●●	Best of …
☼	Scenic view
⊗	Responsible travel: for ecological or fair trade aspects
(*)	Telephone numbers that are not toll-free

**PRICE CATEGORIES
HOTELS**

Expensive	over 120 euros
Moderate	80–120 euros
Budget	under 80 euros

Price for a double room, without breakfast, in the high season

**PRICE CATEGORIES
RESTAURANTS**

Expensive	over 35 euros
Moderate	25–35 euros
Budget	under 25 euros

Prices apply to a menu with a minimum of two courses excluding drinks and beverages

CONTENTS

DID YOU KNOW?
Timeline → p. 14
Local specialities → p. 28
For bookworms and
film buffs → p. 51
The Riviera is making
an effort → p. 71
Public holidays → p. 119
Currency converter → p. 125
Budgeting → p. 126
Weather → p. 127

**MAPS IN THE
GUIDEBOOK**
(134 A1) Page numbers and
coordinates refer to the road
atlas
(0) Site/address located off
the map. Coordinates are
also given for places that are
not marked on the road atlas

(*◻ A–B 2–3*) Refers to
the removable pull-out map

INSIDE FRONT COVER:
The best Highlights

INSIDE BACK COVER:
Maps of Monaco, Nice and
Cannes

The best MARCO POLO Insider Tips

Our top 15 Insider Tips

INSIDER TIP Perfume par excellence

Scent workshop – make your very own perfume at the Galimard perfume factory in Grasse (photo above) → **p. 64**

INSIDER TIP Tranquil travellers' rest

Not only is Auberge du Vieux Château in Cabris a gourmet delight but its lovely canopy beds will have you drifting off to sleep in no time, ahead of another exciting day on the Riviera → **p. 64**

INSIDER TIP A sea view at every turn

One of the most beautiful hiking trails is along the coast on the Giens peninsula. You will need about two hours when you leave from La Madrague yacht harbour → **p. 73**

INSIDER TIP Village dream house

The Bolgari family opens its Maison de Julie in Le Plan near Entrevaux to guests. Beautifully furnished rooms, charmingly arranged details, peace and quiet, and a fabulous breakfast on the terrace → **p. 92**

INSIDER TIP Excellent evening mix

What's it to be: tango, fairytales, punk? They're all at the Court Circuit Café in Nice → **p. 46**

INSIDER TIP Underwater sensation

Snorkel the unique underwater nature trail off Port-Cros, the smallest of the Iles d'Or near Hyères. All you need is a bathing costume and your snorkelling gear → **p. 112**

INSIDER TIP Organic village

It started with the wine growers changing their farming practices. Now the whole village in Correns has switched to organic farming → **p. 90**

INSIDER TIP A touch of the Caribbean

There's a touch of the Caribbean in Provence where the Bresque stream near Sillans-La-Cascade tumbles 40 m/131.2 ft down in a waterfall with a mini jungle around the basin (photo on right) → **p. 92**

BEST OF ...

FOR FREE

● *Free art in Mougins*

Mougins opens the doors to its town museums free of charge, both at the *Museum of Photography* with portraits of Picasso by David Douglas Duncan and at the *Museum* to local artist Maurice Gottlob → p. 61, 62

● *By bus to the hinterland*

Not quite for free, but almost: in the metropolis Nice, ten tickets for the *buses* will set you back only 1 euro. So for 2 euros, you can explore all the pretty villages in the hinterland → p. 48

● *Art ramble on the ramparts*

Amble along the walls of a medieval town while admiring contemporary art at the same time – all for free. In the exclusive *Saint-Paul-de-Vence* (photo) many galleries display their sculptures in the alleyways and on the squares → p. 53

● *Famous fragrances*

A nose for perfume? Then head to Grasse where three famous perfume producers – *Fragonard*, *Galimard* and *Molinard* – offer free tours of their perfume factories → p. 63

● *World stars for free*

Throughout the summer, major music stars come to the *Monte Carlo Sporting Summer Festival* in the tiny principality. Tickets are expensive, but you can party on the beach right next to the concert hall and hear everything just as well. And best of all: it's open air → p. 36

● *Head for the river*

When the traffic is solid by the sea and there's nowhere to park, why not opt for a freshwater pool instead? One of the prettiest natural pools, with free admission as well, is the *Vallon Sourn* on the Argens river near the organic village of Correns → p. 91

●●●● Dots in guidebook refer to 'Best of ...' tips

ONLY IN FRENCH RIVIERA
Unique experiences

● *Luxury car parade*

Curious to know what luxury cars are in demand? Then take a stroll down to the *Casino de Monte Carlo* and you will see the celebrities emerging from their Lamborghinis, Maseratis or Ferraris → p. 34

● *Matisse Museum*

Nice's *Musée Matisse* is dedicated exclusively to the artist and is housed in the villa where he lived. The impressive collection of work spans his career from his early days though to the end of his career → p. 44

● *Magnificent parks*

The splendour of its gardens has always attracted wealthy newcomers to stay on on the French Riviera and the park grounds of the *Villa Ephrussi de Rothschild* (photo) is one of the Cap Ferrat's most spectacular – amble through them enjoy the sea views → p. 49

● *Treasure trove*

You'll find traces of the area's wealthy past in many of the villages in the hinterland. In *Lucéram*, for instance, the Église Sainte-Marguerite houses precious baroque church treasures and masterpieces by the School of Nice that no one would expect to find in this deep province → p. 50

● *Palace hotel by the sea*

Palatial is one superlative that does justice to Nice's extravagant and luxurious *Négresco* hotel. It has been hosting princes, statesmen, celebrities and opera divas since 1913. A drink in the bar will give you a taste of its exclusive atmosphere → p. 47

● *Skiing in the morning, beach in the evening*

The main luxury on the Côte d'Azur is the Alps, which are close by. And to make the most of this, just once in your life take the *Snow bus* from Nice up into the mountains for the slopes, then travel back the same way again for cocktails on the beach → p. 46

● *Shop at leisure*

Tuesday is *market day* in *Cotignac* so why not join the laid back locals and indulge in some leisurely shopping amongst the colourful fruit and vegetable stalls → p. 89

ONLY IN

BEST OF ...

● *Deep sea wonders*
If it is a raining why not let the aquarium brighten up you day. Some 4000 aquatic creatures, fish and coral species are on display at Monaco's *Musée Océanographique* (photo) → p. 35

● *Shop until you drop*
The 100 or so shops and boutiques in Nice's *Nicetoile* shopping mall should keep you busy for at least one rainy afternoon → p. 46

● *A rainy day town*
Biot is the perfect place for a rainy day. If you get caught in a sudden shower, take shelter under one of the Romanesque arcades in the old town. If the rain persists have a coffee at the vaulted Café des Arcades and let the owners show you their art collection. Or spend some time watching the local glass-blowers at work → p. 48

● *Great ride*
Tourists are undoubtedly the most relaxed people on the *Train des Pignes*: all the others are commuters. When it rains, you can watch the Var river rise in minutes as the tracks almost disappear under the water → p. 93

● *The sands of time*
Tende's *Musée des Merveilles* has a way of making the time simply fly by on a rainy day, transporting you back in time to the origins of civilization → p. 85

● *Sweet bombs*
Have you ever held a clementine that seems to weigh a tonne in your hand? No? Then head to *Florian*. At their shop in Pont-du-Loup you'll see how the fruit is dipped in sugar to make it heavy and sweet → p. 31

RAIN

RELAX AND CHILL OUT
Take it easy and spoil yourself

● Chilling without sand
It doesn't always have to be the beach. If you've got children with you, you're sure to enjoy a relaxed afternoon amongst the water features of the *Promenade du Paillon*, the new park at the heart of Nice. Lay a blanket on the ground, unpack your *pan bagnat* and watch your offspring at play in the water → **p. 45**

● Wellness well deserved
Enjoy the rejuvenating effects of seawater pools and other spa treatments at the *Thermes Marins* next to Monaco's Grande Casino. The treatments come at a price but with a bit of luck you can get your money back at the gambling tables later on → **p. 36**

● Oasis of peace and quiet
If you need to get away from it all then a stay at the monastery on the island *Saint-Honorat* is for you. The last ferry leaves the small island just off Cannes at 6pm and then the only sounds are prayer, meditation and the sound of the sea (photo) → **p. 61**

● Spa treatments from the Far East
Asia's latest spa trends are also available on the Riviera. Whether it is a shiatsu massage or a Chinese *tuina* massage, a treatment at *Monte Carlo Spa Mirabeau* in Monaco or *Le Velvet Room* in Juan-les-Pins will leave you feeling as though you have just returned from a trip to the Far East → **p. 18**

● Just like the good old days
Pissaladière, stuffed vegetables (petits farcis), homemade gnocchi, tasty tripe – you can still enjoy Nice's old specialities like in the old days: on the terrace of the *Brasserie de L'Union* in the university district Borriglione, far from the tourist bustle → **p. 46**

● Escape the traffic
In summer the only road leading to Saint-Tropez is jam-packed. Why not set out from *Sainte-Maxime* with the ferry instead. This also means that the money you would have spent on expensive parking can now be better spent at one of the lovely cafés → **p. 79**

INTRODUCTION

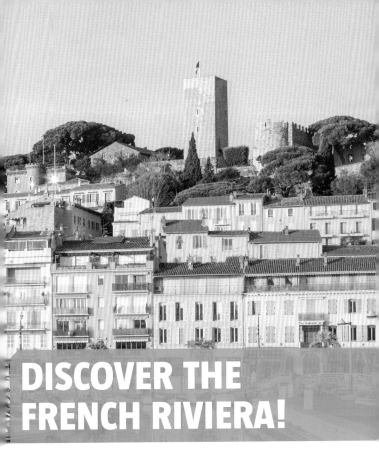

DISCOVER THE FRENCH RIVIERA!

Sizzle on the beach until your skin glows, then a few hours later don your *hiking boots to climb a 2000-m/6600-ft peak*. Or sip champagne in a luxurious restaurant by the sea, then head for an isolated mountain village to snooze under the sycamores. The French Riviera or the Côte d'Azur is a *region of contrasts* that only combined provide a true picture of a region that offers its visitors virtually unlimited holiday choice between the sea and mountain peaks. The mild Mediterranean climate and its many hours of sunshine attract millions of visitors a year to the Riviera. They are also the reasons why Grasse, the *world's perfume capital*, found its niche here and why more than 20,000 people choose to work in the Sophia Antipolis *technology park* outside Antibes. The magnificent Riviera is a *world leader in international tourism*.

What's the betting that only a few decades ago you would not have recognised the coast between Toulon in the west, Menton in the east and the *Parc National du Mercantour* in the north? Back then, the slopes down to the sea were just impenetrable undergrowth of thorny bushes, the villages grey-stoned fortresses. The farmers and fishermen probably never dreamt that their poor land would ever be

---

Photo: The old harbour of Cannes

Coming in February? By all means – that's when the Côte celebrates its wonderful mimosas and lemons

worth so much. And then word got around that the *sun also shone in winter*, that the sea was a turquoise shimmer, and that the local olives and tomatoes were delicious. But because tourists love the sea and the beach more than anything else, the hinterland hasn't changed that much: in some villages such as Bormes-les-Mimosas and Sainte-Agnès, no one would turn an eye if a horse-drawn cart were to turn around the corner. The French still play boules on the market squares today, and drink their *ice-cold*

French Riviera – the land of two thousand opportunities

pastis. There are no ugly new buildings, and none of the usual shops you see everywhere. Saorge in the Roya valley and La Garde-Freinet in the Massif des Maures were *woken from their deep* blow by new residents that had both money and

2800–1300 BC
Rock paintings in the Vallée des Merveilles north of Nice are evidence of Bronze Age settlements

4th century BC
Nikaia (Nice) and Antipolis (Antibes) founded by the Greeks

49 BC
Julius Caesar establishes Forum Julii (Fréjus) after the conquest of Gaul

6 BC
Romans raise victory monument in La Turbie after subjugating the Alpine tribes

1297
François Grimaldi conquers the castle of Monaco (The Prince's Palace)

taste – today both villages epitomise stylishness with no expense spared. Then there are also *villages* like Villecroze a beautifully restored, flower-bedecked idyll with pretty squares and fountains.

Today the Côte d'Azur or French Riviera is synonymous with a leisure-loving society. All that counts is the *here and now*: the azure sea, blue skies and sunshine – 271 days a year. Hyères, Nice and Cannes were the *first ever international holiday destination*. The European aristocracy followed suit, arriving to seek refuge from dire winters and making the Riviera their playground. This high society would become instrumental in turning the region into the *artistic 'garden of Eden'* that it is today. In 1857 the locals looked on in disbelief as Parisian botanist Gustave Thuret began cultivating palms, cacti, cypresses and eucalyptus trees at Cap d'Antibes. Today the exotic *mimosa trees* (an import and not indigenous) make a deep yellow flower spectacle in late winter. They are as integral to the identity of the Riviera today as are the azure blue sea, the deep green *Aleppo pines* and the bright yellows of Menton's *lemon trees*.

> **A playground for an eccentric and extravagant aristocracy**

Complementing this lavish flora is the coast's *architecture*. The *cosmopolitan chic in-crowd* of yesteryear built their palatial abodes without taking into account the architectural styles of the day. And there are numerous examples of this. For instance, the Casino of Monte Carlo, designed by Charlers Garnier of Paris Opera House fame, which looks like any princess's dream with its white stucco and ceiling paintings. And the Hotel Négresco in Nice, with its pink-and-turquoise cupola that is not unlike a sugary cake. And the *modernist villa* built for the Noaille family in Hyères.

An important time in the history of the French Riviera has to be the *belle époque* that began in the early 20th century – *in the winter*. It is hard to believe that it was only in 1931 that a number of courageous hotel owners opened their doors in the summer months for the first time. That season was too hot for the old aristocracy but today the Riviera lives off *summer tourism*. In July and August everything is *in full swing* and packed to the hilt – its restaurants, clubs, streets, hotels,

1789 After the French revolution the principality of Monaco is annexed as Fort Hercules and after Napoléon's conquest of Nice becomes part of the Département Alpes-Maritimes

1815 Napoléon lands in Golfe-Juan on 1 March. Napoléon's Hundred Days end with the Battle of Waterloo

1878 Charles Garnier builds the Monte Carlo Casino

1944 Allies liberate the French Riviera

camping sites and magnificent bays. Prices rise as fast as the temperatures and you will struggle to find parking near famous beaches like Saint-Tropez. Once an inconspicuous fishing village, Impressionist artists put it on the map around 1900 and in 1950 it became synonymous with the *international jet set*. The first iconic figures to arrive were authors from Paris, followed by a variety of French celebrities like Roger Vadim and Brigitte *Bardot* and Johnny Hallyday. Johnny still comes to the beach bars of Pampelonne and Tahiti, as does U2 singer Bono, and lots of models berth their yachts here. Best of all: even non-VIPs can afford at least a soft drink there – and there's no charge at all for the fine sand.

The Saint-Tropez peninsula Ramatuelle stands again for *new developments*: it is campaigning against mass tourism. Drastic new building restrictions have been imposed to conserve the beauty of the coastal strip and its stunning natural landscape. Even though it may seem unlikely, there are still a few *isolated and secluded bays* to swim in even in peak season. Despite the fact that the Saint-Tropez peninsula is the playground of Europe's multi-millionaires, its *beaches are all open* to the public. These beaches, where the offspring of the wealthy hold their champagne parties today, are set to be future *models for nature conservation and environmental protection*. *Conservatoire du Littoral* is making it its mission to save in Saint-Tropez that which has already been lost between Cannes and Nice. This has come about thanks to the awareness that there is more to this coastline than a leisure seeking paradise for a few months of the year. Instead it is a gift of nature whose fauna and flora must be respected and conserved.

> Today, everything that can be organic is organic – even the hair colours used by the hairdressers

This environmental awareness also infiltrated the agricultural sector with wine makers being the first to *reject pesticides and artificial fertilizers* in favour of organic methods. The most striking success story is the village of Correns whose wine farming mayor, Michael Latz, changed over to organic farming for economic reasons. By changing to organic cultivation, the viticulturists of the hinterland opened up a previously untapped niche market. Today they are the proud producers be-

1946 First film festival in Cannes

1969 Foundations laid for the Sophia Antipolis Technology Park in the Antibes hinterland

2003 Almost 50,000 acres of forest burn in the hottest summer in recent decades

2014 Birth of heir to the throne Jacques and his twin sister Gabriella in the Principality of Monaco

2017 On 14 July, people in the South of France remember the victims of the Nice lorry attack the year before

hind the Correns label sold at affordable prices across Europe. Nowadays most of the produce from Correns is organic and its markets are *full of once-forgotten fruits and vegetables* – tomatoes and apricots have never tasted better! Now everything is organic: even the hairdressers use natural hair dyes.

Away from the coast is the *grandiose splendour* of the deep *gorges* that the *Verdon*, Var, Loup and Roya rivers have carved into the rocky terrain. From the spectacular bright red rock Gorges du Cians it is only a short stretch to the Mercantour National Park – where *wolves have made a comeback* – and then it is only a two-hour drive to the coastline and its chic beaches.

Always follow the sea – best views for walkers

Discover the French Riviera's coastline and *three of France's most beautiful départements* (administrative regions): Alpes-Maritimes, Var and Alpes-de-Haute-Provence. Hugging the coast, this travel guide will take you on a journey from Toulon to Menton and both motorists and hikers alike are in for some very spectacular sights. Département Var is home to a stretch of over 250 km/155 mi of the *sentier littoral*, the *coastal hiking trail* between Bandol and Saint-Raphaël. So pack your hiking boots and swimming costume and explore the azure coast of contrasts!

Exploring the tiny old streets of Saint-Paul de Vence

WHAT'S HOT

1 Locavore

Shop locally, dine locally Lemons right outside the front door, tomatoes in the garden and beer from the neighbour's cellar: people in the South of France know that the best food is produced right outside their own front doors. Available, naturally, on all the local markets – and in the brand new shop *Jean la Tomate (closed Sun/Mon | 3, Rue Tonduti-de-l'Escarène)* in Nice. Apart from that – keep your eyes peeled! Signs such as *faite maison* – homemade – and *cuisine nissarde* advertise that the meals served in the pubs and restaurants really are freshly cooked and local.

Asian import 2

Wellness The newest 🌐 spa trend, is a concept imported from the Far East. So embrace the trend and treat yourself to a shiatsu massage at *Monte Carlo Spa Mirabeau (2, Av. de Monte-Carlo | Monaco | www.thermesmarinsmontecarlo.com)* or relieve your tension with a Chinese *tuina* massage at *Le Velvet Room (67, Blvd. Raymond Poincaré | Juan-les-Pins | www.levelvetroom.com)*.

Iron John & Co.

3

Run for your life Hot soles guaranteed: there's lots of running on the French Riviera – quarter, half and full marathons, trails and Ironman, as well as climbing and hiking over all of the peaks in the nearby Maritime Alps. Extreme athletes have now discovered this sunny area for themselves. One highlight is the "vertical kilometre" in Saint-Martin-Vésubie in June, when participants have to ascend 1100 altitude metres/3609 feet over just 4 km/2.5 mi – very short; sweet is debatable. The season ends in November with three different trails at Saint-Jeannet – those who feel like it can run a marathon over the pretty town's mountain ranges.

Snow fun

Skijoring The French Riviera recently been turned upside down: more and more sun-worshippers are heading for the hills and the snow between November and April. The peaks of the Mercantour National Park are 1800 m/5900 ft high and if you like the idea of skiing without exerting yourself then skijoring is for you. It is a form of cross-country skiing where horses or dogs draw you along on your skis. In Valdeblore Marc Ducrez offers a horse drawn option *(La Colmiane, www.colmiane.com)* while in Castérino you can enjoy pristine nature with a husky sleigh ride *(Roya Bévéra, www.sherpamerveilles.com)*. More information on winter sports at *www.cotedazur-neige.com*

Glamping

Camping in style is the upmarket holidaymaker's answer to communing with nature without having to rough it. It is called glamping and with the French Riviera being synonymous with style, it comes as no surprise that the concept quickly took hold. At *Riviera Village (Route des Plages | Ramatuelle | www.riviera-villages.com) (photo)* you can stay in a Polynesian themed chalet that comes with every comfort including air conditioning and satellite television. Another unusual option is *Terre d'Arômes (Séranon, www.terre-d-aromes.com)* which offers luxury yurts in the mountains. At the four-star *Les Tournels* camping village, the huts have an amazing view of the bay of Pampelonne and can accommodate up to six persons *(Route de Camarat | Ramatuelle | www.tournels.com)*.

IN A NUTSHELL

SPEED RUSH

The tightest curve in Formula 1 racing is still in Monaco: a short distance from the Casino of Monte-Carlo is the "bottleneck", which has racing drivers hitting the brakes. In May, the mini state with the city circuit of 1911 is overrun by racing fans. And as if that weren't enough, the name of one of the most renowned car manufacturers in the world was invented on the French Riviera. Entrepreneur Emil Jellinek, who lived in Nice, wanted a memorable name for the vehicles of the wealthy gentlemen drivers. And so he named the cars that were already racing over the mountain roads of the South of France coast at the beginning of the 20th century after his daugher Mercedes. It's not known whether he asked her first.

RURAL & DELICIOUS

A caraffe of wine, checked tablecloths. Fresh ratatouille. And you have the kind of bistro that visitors like. Since 1992 the "Bistrot de Pays", i.e. the rural guesthouses, have been subsidised by the government. After all, the country inns in the tiny villages are an important part of their cultural heritage.

The concept is straightforward and incentive driven. The population of the village where the candidate bistro (restaurant or café) is situated may not exceed 2000. It has to be one of the few of its kind in the area and be open all year round. It has to serve regional cuisine and be a tourism centre by offering local maps, bread, fresh produce or other local specialities. Thanks to the programme, more than a

Photo: Ingredients for perfume at Molinard

Ra... / ...tchouli ATCHOULI / Encens FRANCKINCENSE / Mousse de chêne OAK MOSS

...ICHEN / GOMME / ...OUSSE

It is not all beaches, glitz, glamour and promenades – the cosmopolitan French Riviera has something for everyone

hundred of such restaurants especially in the Nice hinterland, in the Cotignac area of Provence and in the Verdon valley are now ranked among southern France's best. For the complete list go to *www. bistrotdepays.com*.

W ELL-PRESERVED NATURE

Most people dream of a house by the seaside but on the French Riviera this dream has also had an ugly downside with some densely built up sections.

The worst affected stretch is the one between Cannes and Monaco, where architectural monstrosities and private beaches obscure the view of the sea. After years of this building free for all, the state finally introduced the *Conservatoire du Littoral* in 1975. This conservation body has since managed to protect more than 35,000 acres of land in Provence and the Riviera from real estate developers, along with more than 100 km/62 mi of coastline. In 1989 the association also succeeded in buying

Keep your eyes peeled: on every street corner in Cannes you'll bump into some big name from the film industry

Domaine du Rayol between Bormes-les-Mimosas and the Saint-Tropez peninsula – much sought after by developers. The landscape architect Gilles Clément then transformed the botanical garden and arboretum in to a nature trail of trees, shrubs and flowers from around the world. The *Conservatoire* is also responsible for the coastal hiking trails, the *sentier littoral* is another example of the conservation drive. These paths fulfil a legal requirement by making a 3 m/9.8 ft wide strip along the sea accessible to the general public. This means that some of the most scenic coastal hiking trails in France can be found in the Cap d'Antibes peninsula or in Cap Martin in Monaco or along the Saint-Tropez peninsula. One exception: pedestrians are not permitted to walk through Brigitte Bardot's front garden – her property enjoys a special status.

SUMMIT MEETING

Cannes is synonymous with Europe's most prestigious film festival and every May its Palme d'Or (awarded in the Croisette since 1946) turns Cannes into a rendezvous for stars and starlets from around the world. Fans and onlookers brave the throng and flock there for the chance of catching a glimpse of their favourite celebrities as they make their way along the red carpet up the gigantic flight of stairs to the Festival Hall.

CULTURE OF WELCOME

Did you know that only messy scrub and stunted oak trees are native to the French Riviera? Everything else that grows here – the stately date palms, the gnarled olives trees and the numerous fragrant lemon trees – were brought here in recent centuries from

ple in the South of France were nourished by olives. For many centuries, people on the coast and in the surrounding villages lived off this "black gold", as it is called there. Olive trees need colder winter days for the fruits to develop, but they also need the heat in summer – the climate in the Maritime Alps is ideal for them. Even if they're not native to the French Mediterranean.

M EGALOMANIA

Where there's money, megalomania isn't far behind. The French Riviera is continuing to develop a shopping imperium that is pretty well beyond compare. *Cap3000* in Nice has now acquired new neighbours in the form of the *Polygone Riviera* in Cagnes-sur-Mer, and Cannes is also already working on its next mall. Even though Cannes has mostly international brands, the fountains and palms add a South Sea flair to this over-sized haven of window shopping. However, even these modern shopping centres are harmless compared with what former town leaders had planned: such as the artificial three-story island off Cannes. A 22-acre pyramid with 600 hotel beds, three swimming pools and 8000 cinema seats was to rise out of the water directly in front of the Croisette. The island was to be mobile, sometimes anchoring off the western hill of the old town, others on the eastern end of the Croisette. In the days when Jacques Médecin, who was later wanted internationally for various misdemeanours, was still mayor of Nice, the craziest ideas simply tumbled out of the town hall. Médecin wanted to move traffic from the beach promenade onto a dual carriageway into the sea. Cars were to drive around 50 m/164 ft from the coast, and the beach would be turned into a lagoon with views of a

countries even further south. Today, the palm trees flank every beach promenade, and orange and lemon trees can be found in every garden. The bitter varieties even grow in the shopping precincts, although they're usually only ornamental. Try one, and your mouth will just pucker up – as it will if you try an olive raw straight from the tree; they are almost unbelievably bitter. But oh! The oil – what a delight! Kilos of the tiny black fruits fall from the trees in Nice. Olive trees are fabulous. They can live to be a thousand years old. And they are impressive survivors: saw the trunk 1 m/3.3 ft from the ground, and in the following year you'll find countless new branches. Even trees that froze above the ground in the now legendary cold of the winter of 1985 were revived by ground shoots. No wonder that peo-

motorway. Fortunately, both the Cannes island and the sea motorway off Nice's promenade came to nought.

MAKE IT BIGGER

Hypermarché is the concept that combines the supermarket and department store in one massive floor space area with an almost boundless product selection. These colossal bastions of consumerism can be found in all of the major towns and cities and even some of the smaller municipalities and despite being architectural eyesores, they are very popular with locals and tourists alike. You will be spoilt for choice with row upon row of just about any product you can think of. It is best to allow yourself plenty of time and to make an outing of it. But, if the thought of pushing a shopping trolley from aisle to aisle sounds like a chore then rather head straight to the delicatessen or pastry counter and indulge in something delicious. Big hypermarché names like Carrefour, Leclerc, Auchan, Casino or Intermarché are a gourmet delight.

THE VISIT FROM THE LITTLE MAN

France's most famous strategist experienced some of the biggest highs and lows of his career on the Mediterranean coast. In 1793, at the age of 24, Napoléon experienced his first victory with the siege of Toulon after he liberated the town from its English occupiers. A year later Napoléon was stationed as a general in Nice which is where he set off from on his Italian campaign in 1796. In 1799, after his Egypt expedition, he was back on the French Riviera in Saint-Raphaël and it was from here that he would go into exile on Elba 15 years later. Not quite a year later he returned to Golfe-Juan and celebrated his triumphant return to Paris on the Alpine Route Napoléon of today.

A FRAGRANT BUSINESS

Orange blossoms, jasmine, lavender, roses and violets – these are the fragrances that have made Grasse the perfume capital of the world as far back as the 16th century. The orange blossoms come from the coast, the herbs from the mountains, the violets from Tourrettes-sur-Loup and the jasmine and roses from Grasse itself. Today the fragrances and flavourings created for the cosmetics and food industry constitutes half the turnover of the 30 or more companies involved in the industry.

P FOR PAPPS

Paparazzi, pop stars, poodles and professionals – so many Ps on the coast in summer. The more expensive the place, the more big names there will be. If you want to see Madonna, Paris Hilton, Adele and Jayzee with oversized shades and the opligatory pooch, you'll have to head for Cap Ferrat or Saint-Tropez, where you'll see them in the restaurants – unless they're hiding behind high walls and uniformed security guards. Others head for the tax haven Monaco, rubbing shoulders with racing drivers and tennis greats. When Leonardo di Caprio or Bono take a yacht to Pampelonne's beach restaurant nobody bats an eyelid. However, with Saint-Tropez Mayor Jean-Pierre Tuveri counting 30,000 helicopter charters over his area alone last summer, it does seem that celebrities are becoming a bit of a problem in this idyllic part of the world.

OLD MASTERS, NEW MASTERS

The *École de Nice* style was founded by Louis Bréa in the 15th century in the French

Riviera. Sadly Bréa's fame did not reach beyond the borders of France but there has recently been a renewed interest in the works of baroque artists. Churches with art works by Louis Bréa, his brother Antoine and his nephew François can be seen in Nice (Cimiez Monastery), Sospel (Saint-Michel), La Brigue (Saint-Martin), Coursegoules (Sainte-Marie-Madeleine) and in Lucéram (Sainte-Marguerite).

But the art scene on the French Riviera did not rest on the laurels of its ancestors. Yves Klein from Nice (who died in 1962) was one of the founders of New Realism and

SAVE RESOURCES? NO, THANK YOU!

Guess what the most expensive thing about a yacht is. No, it's not the crew, nor is it the shiny chrome on deck. Quite simply, it's the fuel. For the short trip from Nice to Monaco – a distance of only 20 km/12.4 mi – a medium-sized boat will consume the unbelievable – and environ-mentally-unfriendly – amount of 200 litres of fuel. Which gives you some idea of how much these boats actually cost their owners. The biggest private yachts drop anchor off Saint-Tropez or Monaco.

When is peak season in Saint-Tropez? When you can't see the harbour for yachts

other artists like Arman (from Nice) and Martial Raysse (from Golfe-Juan) were also part of the movement. Artists of the modern *École de Nice* who made a name for themselves are Niki de Saint-Phalle, Daniel Spoerri Ben Vautier and Claude Vialet.

If they are allowed. Often, even bil-lionaires have to wait years for a moor-ing on the French Riviera. But then they will be able to clink champagne glasses with Paris Hilton, Heidi Klum or a Saudi Arabian king on the luxury liner next door.

FOOD & DRINK

Dolce vita, or the life of Riley? Oh, just have it all on the French Riviera: the tastiest from Italy, well combined with specialities from the South of France. Everything here is a touch finer than the down-to-earth cuisine you experience elsewhere: the tiny tartes, the towers of vegetables and, of course, the squid salad and vegetable ratatouille.

The French Riviera's cuisine is simple, light and healthy with a large variety of *vegetables*, *fish* and *shellfish*, and a selection of *herbs* such as thyme, rosemary, mint, sage, basil, fennel and bay leaves. In addition there is lamb from the highlands, goat or sheep's milk cheeses, exotic fruits, and last but not least its local *wines* – a regional success story.

The emphasis here is always on fresh produce. In winter, the south of France hosts a famous *truffle market* – held in Aups north of the Département Var. The stretch between Toulon and Menton is where an increasing number of farmers are going organic. The tiny village of Correns in the Var hinterland is the best example of this new approach and its entire wine, vegetable and fruit production is organic. The produce from these relatively small farms are sold at specialist markets or *marchés paysans* or they are snapped up by top restaurants.

Despite fast food becoming increasingly popular – especially among the youth – in the bigger cities, there is hardly any other region in France with as many *Michelin star chefs* as on the French

Bild: Goat's cheese specialities

The sea and the farms all provide the best ingredients for the light unpretentious cuisine of the south

Riviera. 'Simplicity and luxury are the principles that define Provençal cuisine', is what Alain Ducasse – who has built up his empire of top restaurants from his Restaurant Le Louis XV in the Hôtel de Paris in Monaco – has to say. His mentor was Roger Vergé, who is considered to be the father of the *cuisine du sud*. It seems that these haute cuisine masters tend to stick to *simple recipes*. If you think about it, all that sun-kissed tomatoes and courgettes need for their fragrant flavours to unfold is a *touch of* *fresh herbs* and a dash of olive oil. Fresh vegetables like these and fish, olive oil, garlic and good wines are the reasons behind the fact that the people from the south have the highest life expectancy in France.

Even visitors on a tight budget will find that reasonably priced *good regional cuisine* is easy to come by, both on the coast or in the hinterland villages.

Although the French are great chefs, when it comes to organic, vegan or vegetarian cuisine, *they're a few years*

LOCAL SPECIALITIES

aïoli – a mayonnaise made from garlic, egg yolk and olive oil. Usually served on a Friday with cod *(morue)*, hard boiled eggs and carrots *(carottes)*, potatoes *(pommes de terre)* and sometimes green beans *(haricots verts)*

bouillabaisse – fish soup made of scorpion fish *(rascasse)*, gurnard *(grondin)* and sea eel *(congre)*. Other ingredients include onions, tomatoes, saffron, garlic, bay leaf, fennel, sage, orange zest and of course olive oil

bourride – similar to a bouillabaisse, but with sea bass *(loup)*, monkfish *(baudroie)* and whiting *(merlan)* and thickened with aïoli

estocaficada – stockfish slowly stewed with tomatoes, onions, peppers, potatoes and a blend of herbs, garnished with black olives

fleurs de courgette – stuffed courgette flowers

pan bagnat – a baguette sandwich with a filling of lettuce leaves, raw onions, tomatoes, anchovies, black olives and boiled egg

petits farcis – stuffed vegetables e. g. courgettes, tomatoes or aubergines

pissaladière – onion tart featuring *pissala*, a thick anchovy-based sauce and black olives (photo left)

ratatouille – a vegetable dish of aubergines, peppers, tomatoes, onions and courgettes, braised in olive oil and garlic, served hot or cold (photo right)

salade niçoise – tuna salad on a bed of lettuce, green beans, radishes, black olives, green peppers, hard boiled eggs, anchovies and an olive oil dressing

socca – chickpea flatbread baked in a large pan

soupe au pistou – vegetable soup of white beans, tomatoes and courgettes (often cooked with bacon) served with a dollop of *pistou* a thick paste of basil, garlic and olive oil

tapenade – a rich spread of black olives, capers and anchovy fillets

tian de légumes – sliced vegetables such as aubergines, spinach, white beans or courgettes baked in a *tian* – the name given to the flat oven-proof earthenware dishes of southern France

tourta de blea – sweet cake made of chard *(blettes)* with pine kernels and raisons

behind. Even today, they still think a meal isn't a meal without meat. And yet some people are already starting to do without meat or even entirely without food of animal origin. *Vegan restaurants* are seen alongside the omnipresent butchers. Like the *Vegan Gorilla* in Nice, for instance, or brunchy *Arts Thés Miss* in Antibes. Some even have uncooked dishes for adherents to the *raw food movement*. Usually they're organic and local as well – and no one misses the otherwise almost obligatory lamb shank.

The French don't eat meat for breakfast *(petit déjeuner)* anyway; to them it's rather adventurous. Instead, it's a very frugal meal: *café au lait* served with a baguette or a croissant (if you are lucky) with butter and jam, but the French *lunch (déjeuner)* served between noon and 2pm will certainly make up for this as it is a hearty *three course set menu*. This meal is integral to the French way of life and includes a starter *(hors d'œuvre)*, main course *(plat de résistance)* of either meat *(viande)*, fish *(poisson)* or poultry *(volaille)* rounded off by dessert. In keeping with changing times, restaurants will not mind if you simply order a salad main or if you opt for the special of the day *(plat du jour)*. It is at *dîner* or *souper* (seldom before 8pm) that the Riviera's cuisine *really comes into its own*. Set aside a good few hours, so you can enjoy the entire experience starting with the appetiser *(amuse-gueule)* and making your way right through to the signature lemon peel *(zeste de citron)* you will find on your dessert platter.

A basket of French bread and a carafe of water come standard with meals and are free of charge. Splitting the bill is frowned upon on the French Riviera where it is customary to have a bill per table.

Tiny region, fabulous wine: a *Bellet* from the north of Nice

Many restaurants in the region now have their own cellars of locally produced wine. Wines from the *Bellet* region in the north of Nice are cultivated on 1700 acres of wine lands and have been awarded the AOC since 1941, that has been renamed AOP *(Appelation d'Origine Protégée)* in 2011. Wine farmers like the de Charnacé family at Château de Bellet cultivate red wines from old grape varieties like *Folle Noire* and *Braquet*.

SHOPPING

Luxury, style and elegance are what has epitomised the French Riviera's coastal towns and villages for over a century and the sky is the limit here when it comes to shopping. Its international reputation means that just about every high-end brand can be found in its boutiques. But the French Riviera also has its own specialities such as the perfumes from Grasse which make excellent souvenirs.

FASHION

Which outfit is the most important on the French Riviera? A bikini, of course! That's why these tiny textile teasers are now being created by new designers between Saint-Tropez and Menton. Such as *Kiwi*, for instance, with its imaginative prints (watermelons, bathing nymphs) or *Val d'Azur* in many of the shops that are so golden and shiny and kinky that they hurt your eyes ...

GLASSWARE

Biot is a delightfully picturesque hilltop village with a rich artistic heritage and an international reputation for its glass making. It has no less than eight glass making studios. The largest and oldest of these are *La Verrerie de Biot (Chemin des Combes | www.verreriebiot.com)* and the atelier of *Raphaël Farinelli*: *La Verrerie Farinelli (465, Route de la Mer | www.farinelli.fr)*, an Italian whose glass art is exceptional.

LOCAL MARKETS

Note: We're not talking about the fruit and vegetable stands that flog only Spanish greenhouse cucumbers in the tourist zones, but the *marché paysan* or *marché producteur*, which has finally been reintroduced everywhere and sells local vegetables along with lambswool jumpers, leather sandals and handmade pottery bowls. Everything is locally made – so it's guaranteed not to be a tourist trap.

PORCELAIN

Moustiers-Sainte-Marie has a rich history in porcelain craftsmanship and decoration and is home to a dozen workshops *(www.moustiers.eu)*. The craft is experiencing a renaissance because it is once again trendy to serve regional dishes in traditional Provençal tableware.

A shoppers' paradise: upscale designer boutiques and shops on the coast and a selection of fine crafts in the hinterland

SWEETS

In a region where lemons and oranges thrive, there is no shortage of ingredients to make top quality sweets. Highly recommended: *Maison Herbin's* home-made jams/jellies *(2, Rue du Vieux Collège | www.confitures-herbin.com) in* Menton as well as *Maison Auer's* glacéd fruit *(7, Rue Saint-François de Paule | www.maison-auer.com) in* Nice and *Confiserie Florian's* crystallised violet blossoms (see p. 100) at the branch in Nice *(14, Quai Papacino)* or at ● Pont-du-Loup, where you can watch flowers and fruits being turned into sweet temptations.

WINE

With more than 2700 hours a year of sunshine, ample rain and good soil, conditions here are ideal for vineyards and the area produces excellent dry and full-bodied wines. The estates are well worth a visit but for those who prefer convenience there are cooperatives like the *Maison des Vins* in Les Arcs *(RN 7 | www.caveaucp.fr)*. It sells more than 600 different wines from *Côtes de Provence* – a controlled region of origin appellation – without a markup. Their multilingual staff are knowledgeable and helpful and will even offer advice on the lesser known estates. The wines from the vineyards of Nice's hinterland are special in their own right. They are grown in an area of only 120 acres and are identifiable by their distinctive *Vins de Bellet (www.vinsdebellet.com)* wine of origin appellation.

There is an increasing trend among the wine farmers in the *Côteaux Varois* region around Brignoles to go organic. Their wines are sold at the ● *Maison des Vins (tel. 04 94 69 33 18 | www.coteaux-varois.com)* next to Abbaye de La Celle.

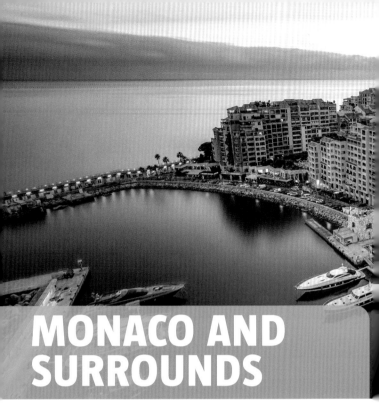

MONACO AND SURROUNDS

MAP INSIDE BACK COVER
(137 D6) *(P–Q6)* **If Cannes is as secure as a bank, then Monaco is Fort Knox. The princely state between Nice and Italy has its very own laws. Anyone the white-gloved gendarmes on the access roads don't like the look of is taken out of circulation. Young people on mopeds, for instance. But don't worry – tourists are usually able to enter the tiny (only 512 acres) state. And then are amazed by the number of billionaires from all over the world who allow themselves to be squeezed into the concrete castles just to save a bit of tax.**

Skyscrapers 20, 30 even 40 storeys high are arranged around the steep slopes like an amphitheatre. Many of them are grey with orange balconies no bigger than 45 ft². And because every building tries to tower over all the others, most people only get to look at concrete; only the lucky tenants on the top floor and in the houses in the harbour still have a sea view. If the small state ever has to charge normal taxes, the skyscrapers would soon be empty. And yet Monaco is attractive. Several hundred people apply for Monagesque nationality every year; only between 10 and 50 of them actually get it. Like Alain Ducasse, for instance, the starred chef who is opening restaurants all over the world, and is *chef de cuisine* at the elegant Hôtel de Paris next door to the Casino of Monaco.

The Casino and the expansive area outside represent the lovely sides on Monaco. The principality is a show, a spruced-up

An oasis for millionaires: this tiny Grimaldi family principality is a tax haven and an economic giant

CITY **WHERE TO START?**

Casino or Rock: if the Rock of Monaco *(Le Rocher)* with the old town, palace and Musée Océanographique is first on your itinerary it is best to leave your car at the *Pêcheurs (max. height 1.90 m/6.2 ft)* or *La Digue* car parks. If you want to head straight to the glamorous casino and shopping area, use the *Casino (maximum height 2 m/6.6 ft)* car park.

Disneyland for the rich. You won't see chewing gum on the pavements; the façades are freshly painted, and signposts instruct tourists not to walk around the old town in bathing shorts. 500 video cameras and 500 policemen watch over Monaco and its 35,000 residents, many more than in other cities of this size. Everything is spotlessly clean.

There are unusual plants in the parks, the cars are highly polished. Exclusive boutiques invite you if not to shop, then to window shop. And since popular Prince

Albert II married the wiry high-performance swimmer Charlene and the two produced twins, the mini state now finally also has its own royal offspring. Only a very few people stand a chance of becoming their neighbours: a minuscule garage in Monaco can cost an unbeliev-

If you lose all your money at the Casino, you can always hock the Ferrari

able 200,000 euros, a one-room apartment a cool million. Wealthy French, Americans or Italians will exchange a tiny apartment for vast tax advantages. Of course, most of them don't actually live in the Mongesque rooms, but a few hours' drive away in a large villa with gardens and a pool. It is said that some rich people even employ others to use electricity for them and convince the tax authorities that they are living a normal life in Monaco.

SIGHTSEEING

OLD TOWN MONACO

Discover the old town by taking a stroll through its narrow, picturesque alleyways: the *Placette Bosio* named after the Monégasque sculptor; the 16th century red brick pedestrian link, the *Rampe Major;* the gardens of *Saint-Martin* with its paths along the south-western face of the Rock of Monaco where a bronze memorial pays tribute to Prince Albert I and the *Cathedrale de Monaco* with *Les Tombes des Princes* where Grace Kelly and Prince Rainier III were laid to rest.

CASINO DE MONTE CARLO ★ ●

A beacon of light in the midst of all the concrete: The gambling halls with their high, decorative windows and bronze chandeliers and the *Salle Garnier* are only open to adults and the admission is 10 euros. The *Jardin du Casino* is a magnificent garden with fountain and the ☙ *Terraces du Casino* has spectacular views of the harbour and the roof of the Congress Centre, designed by the artist Victor Vasarely. *(www. casinomontecarlo.com)*

COLLECTION DE VOITURES ANCIENNES

This museum bears testimony to the Grimaldi's love of cars. Five floors with no less than 100 cars, among them a Bugatti, the winner of the first Formula One race in 1929 and a Rolls Royce Silver Cloud that was a wedding gift to Prince Rainier III and Grace Kelly. *Open daily 10am–6pm | Terrasses de Fontvieille | 6.50 euros*

JARDIN EXOTIQUE ★ ☆

Exotic cacti on the cliff face high above the sea are what make the tropical gardens in the Moneghetti quarter special. The panorama terraces and *Grotte de l'Observatoire,* a picturesque cave 60 m/196.9 ft deep with fossils on display, are the main attractions. There is also the *Musée d'Anthropologie Préhistorique* with its coin and bone collection, and jewellery items. *Mid May–mid Sept daily 9am–7pm, mid Sept–beginning of Nov and end Dec–mid May daily 9am–6pm or as soon as it becomes dark | 7.20 euros | 62, Blvd. du Jardin Exotique | www.jardin-exotique.mc*

MUSÉE OCÉANOGRAPHIQUE ★ ●

Prince Albert I was a passionate oceanographer and the results of his scientific research are on display in the imposing Oceanographic Institute building some 85 m/278.8 ft above the sea. Renowned deep-sea researcher and diver Jacques-Yves Cousteau was director of the Musée Océanographique for 30 years making it world famous. More than 4000 aquatic creatures – giant turtles are some of the oldest – and 200 fish species are on display in over 100 aquariums. Take a ☆ INSIDERTIP break in the caféteria on the roof terrace and enjoy the beautiful sea view. *July/Aug daily 9.30am–7.30pm, April–June and Sept 9.30am–7pm, winter 10am–6pm | admission depending on season 11–16 euros | 2, Av. Saint-Martin | www.oceano.mc*

LE PALAIS PRINCIER

The Prince's Palace is Monaco's royal family home in Monaco Ville – the original fortified town of Monaco. It was built as a Genoese castle in the 13th century and tourists can watch the changing of the guards at the main entrance at 11.55am daily. The palace's *Grands Appartements,* including an Italian gallery, the spectacular throne room and the main courtyard with its Imperial staircase made of Carrara marble, where sometimes concerts are held, are closed in winter. *April–Oct daily 10am–5pm | 8 euros | www.palais.mc*

FOOD & DRINK

ELSA ☺

Chef Paolo Sari has earned himself a Michelin star with his fabulous organic dishes, and cooks up a storm at the Hotel *Monte Carlo Beach (26 rooms | Expensive). Closed Nov–early Mar | Av. Princesse Grace | Roquebrune-Cap-Martin | tel. 98 06 50 05 | www.monte-carlo-beach.com | Expensive*

MARCO POLO HIGHLIGHTS

★ **Casino de Monte Carlo**
Fabulous meeting place for players from all over the world
→ p. 34

★ **Jardin Exotique**
Monaco's exotic garden of rare cacti → p. 35

★ **Musée Océanographique**
Unique perspective on the science of oceanography → p. 35

★ **Saint-Michel-Archange**
Lovely baroque architectural ensemble in Menton → p. 37

★ **Route de la Grande Corniche**
The French Riviera's spectacular scenic route → p. 39

★ **Trophée des Alpes**
Victory monument for Emperor Augustus → p. 39

LE LOUIS XV

Entrepreneur and top chef Alain Duca-sse and his sous chef Franck Cerutti run what is considered to be one of the finest dining establishments in France. It is in opulent belle époque surroundings in the *Hôtel de Paris (143 rooms | tel. 98 06 30 00 | Expensive). Closed on Tue and Wed, also in Dec and Feb–mid-Mar | Place du Casino | tel. 98 06 88 64 | www.alain-ducasse.com | Expensive*

LOW BUDGET

Joss Stone, Tina Turner, Sting, The Cure – world stars are paid a pretty penny for their performances at the ● *Monte Carlo Sporting Summer Festival.* So: slip your shoes off, wriggle your toes in the sand of the neighbouring beach, and listen to the music for free. Is even lovelier and more enjoyable than in the usually overheated hall. Summer programme at *fr.montecarlo live.com*

Located just outside Monaco is *Thalassa hostel (90 beds | 2, av. Gramaglia | Cap d'Ail | tel. 04 93 81 27 63 | www.clajsud.fr)* where accommodation per night in the communal room with sheet and breakfast will cost you 20 euros.

Chef Bruno Cirino of the gourmet establishment *Hostellerie Jérôme* in La Turbie has opened a stylish bistro next to the fountain on the village square that serves simple unpretentious delicacies at affordable prices. *Café de la Fontaine | 4, av. Général de Gaulle | La Turbie | tel. 04 93 28 52 79*

INSIDER TIP MARCHÉ DE LA CONDAMINE

Be like the local builders: eat in the sun at the surprisingly normal prices on the market right at the entrance to Monaco. Or in the market hall, where you will find very tasty, extremely fresh noodle dishes. And *socca*, the chickpea rösti, or the vegetable baguette *pan bagnat. Daily 7am–1pm | Budget*

SHOPPING

Monaco offers everything: from luxury goods and exclusive fashion labels *(Blvd. des Moulins, Av. des Spélugues* or *Av. des Beaux-Arts)* to ordinary everyday items (e. g. *Centre Commercial de Fontvieille).*

SPORTS & BEACHES

Monaco's only swimming beaches are located in the western part of the principality on the Larvotto waterfront.

LES THERMES MARINS

This spa next to the Grand Casino is the ideal relaxation destination. You can enjoy its heated seawater pools, rejuvenating saunas and the spectacular view from the ⤴ fitness studio but it all comes at a price! But you only live once. *7am–9pm daily | 2, Av. de Monte Carlo | tel. 98 06 69 00 | www.thermesmarins montecarlo.com*

ENTERTAINMENT

The VIPs and celebrities hang out in small but exclusive clubs and the meeting places of the in-crowd are *Sass Café (11, Av. Princesse Grace | www.sasscafe. com)* and the tiny *Le Jimmy'z (in summer daily, at other times Wed–Sun from 11pm | reservations essential | evening wear only | 26, Av. Princesse Grace |*

tel. 92 16 22 77 | www.jimmyzmonte carlo.com). Slightly less sophisticated is *Stars 'n' Bars (11am–midnight daily, dancing until 4pm | 6, Quai Antoine 1er | www.starsnbars.com)* with its snack bar, billiard tables, outlandish décor, internet café and concerts. An attraction for 'mere mortals' is the open-air **INSIDER TIP** summer cinema *(Cinéma d'été)* at the *Terrasses du Parking des Pêcheurs* with a screen that is said to be one of the world's largest. *(Every evening end of June–mid Sept | www.cinema2monaco.com)*

93 30 24 64 | www.hoteldefrance.mc | Moderate–Expensive

INFORMATION

22a, Blvd. des Moulins | Monte Carlo | tel. 92 16 61 16 | www.visitmonaco.com

WHERE TO GO

MENTON (137 D–E 5–6) *(𝕸 Q6)*
Italy is right on the doorstep of this quaint south-eastern French town 10 km/6.2 mi

Monaco's construction workers know what's good on the Marché de la Condamine: e.g. *barbagiuan*

WHERE TO STAY

Monaco is very expensive. About 1700 of the 2500 rooms available in Monaco fall in to the luxurious category and are in the palatial hotels surrounding the Grand Casino.

HÔTEL DE FRANCE
Nestled in a quiet alleyway in the suburb of La Condamine near the train station. *26 rooms | 6, Rue de la Turbie | tel.*

east of Monaco with a population of 28,000. In winter, Menton is blessed with some of the best weather on the entire coast. The church square of the basilica of ★ *Saint-Michel-Archange* is regarded as one of the most spectacular examples of the baroque era in the region. Notice how the distinctive Grimaldi coat of arms have been worked into the stone paving.
The *Rue Saint-Michel* shopping promenade takes you through old town Menton

to the *Place aux Herbes* with its street cafés and market hall. *Maison Herbin* is a sheer delight *(guided factory tours Mon, Wed and Fri 10.30am | 2, Rue Palmaro | www.confitures-herbin.com)* with its homemade confitures and variety of pickled vegetables.

In 1958 the artist Jean Cocteau decorated the *Salle des Mariages* (wedding room) of the Menton town hall with his Mon 10am–12.30pm, 3.30pm–6.30pm, Oct–April 10am–12.30pm, 2pm–5pm | 6.50 euros | Av. Saint-Jacques) and the *Jardin Serre de la Madone (closed Nov, Tue–Sun 10am–6pm, in winter 10am–5pm | 8 euros | 74, Route de Gorbio)* planted on the slopes by the Englishman Lawrence Johnston some 100 years ago. The refurbished little *Hôtel Lemon (18 rooms | 10, Rue Albert 1er |*

Menton's arguably prettiest square is in front of the baroque basilica Saint-Michel-Archange

murals *(Mon–Fri 9am–12.30pm, 2pm–5pm | 2 euros | Hôtel de Ville)*. Between the market hall and the sea is Rudy Ricciotti's INSIDERTIP Musée Jean Cocteau *(Wed–Mon 10am–6pm | 8 euros including bastion | 2, Quai de Monléon | museecocteaumenton.fr)* with the 1000 works of American-Belgian entrepreneur Séverin Wunderman's collection.

Menton is also renowned for its exotic tropical gardens like the *Jardin Botanique de Val Rahmeh (May–Sept Wed–* tel. 04 93 28 63 63 | www.hotel-lemon. com | *Budget)* offers inexpensive accommodation. The ◐ organic breakfast is served in the garden. Mauro Colagreco has turned the ◒ *Mirazur (closed Mon, Tue, mid-Nov–mid Feb | 30, Av. Aristide Briand | tel. 04 92 41 86 86 | www.mirazur.fr | Expensive)* close to the Italian border with views of the sea and bay into a gourmet temple. Information: *8, Av. Boyer | tel. 04 92 41 76 76 | www.tourisme-menton.fr*

ROQUEBRUNE-CAP-MARTIN
(137 D5–6) (𝑚 Q6)

The residents are still annoyed about it today: in 1860, they decided to be French rather than belong to the then impoverished Monaco! But Roquebrune also became extremely wealthy without the principality. Even the world-famous architect Le Corbusier once lived here. His weekend house on the beach, the *Cabanon de Le Corbusier,* bears witness to his artistic creativity. The *fortified tower (donjon) (Château | June–Sep daily 10am–1pm, 2.30pm–7pm, otherwise 10am–12.30, 2pm–5pm | 5 euros) dates back to the Middle Ages.* The 26-m/85.3-ft ☀ *lookout platform* offers fabulous views of the village, Cap-Martin and Monaco. The INSIDER TIP *olive tree (Olivier Millénaire)* 200 m/656 ft beyond the village has a 10-m/32.8-ft trunk, and is said to be 4000 years old. Information: *218, Av. Aristide Briand | tel. 04 93 35 62 87 | www.roquebrune-cap-martin.com*

ROUTE DE LA GRANDE CORNICHE ★ ☀
(136–137 C–E 5–6) (𝑚 P–Q6)

This is one of the world's most scenic roads. Napoléon was responsible for building the stretch between Menton and Nice and used some of the existing Roman road, the *Via Julia Augusta.* Winding along at 500 m/1640 ft above the sea the drive has spectacular views of villages, cliffs and the sea. Incidentally, the D 2564 also featured in the 1955 Alfred Hitchcock film *To catch a Thief* with Grace Kelly and Cary Grant. The route goes all the way from Menton via Roquebrune castle to the Roman monument of La Turbie, then from Eze to Nice via the Saint-Jean-Cap-Ferrat peninsula and Villefranche. A word of caution: traffic on this road, on the alternative routes *Moyenne Corniche* (the main road before the motorway was built) and on the *Corniche Inférieure* (built directly along the coastline in the 18th century) can be very heavy in the summer.

SAINTE-AGNÈS (137 D5) (𝑚 Q6)

This mountain village (pop. approx. 1000) 800 m/2625 ft above sea level has a fort *(Jun–Sep daily 10.30am–noon, 3pm–7pm, otherwise Sat/Sun 2pm–5.30pm | 5 euros | wear a jumper in summer as well)* that can be visited with a little shudder: in 1940, French soldiers hid from Italian soldiers for months in the almost windowless rooms hewn into the rocks. After this oppressive sight, the endless ☀ views of the sea are even more welcome. Fewer tourists and pretty cafés make this excursion perfect. Information: *www.sainteagnes.fr*

TROPHÉE DES ALPES ★ ☀
(137 D6) (𝑚 P6)

An interesting Roman building high above Monaco. Emperor Augustus was so proud to have conquered a whole 44 tribes in the Alps that he "gifted" the coast this trophy. Today, though, the memorial is most striking for the contrast that pieces of rock and stone thousands of years old were able to survive just a few feet as the crow flies above the latest architectural wonders of Monaco. And then, in 1929, were rebuilt by American Edward Tuck.

You can learn the complete and extremely varied history of this park-like fortress, which also has a lookout terrace, in the village (pop. 3200) of *La Turbie (5 km/3.1 mi north-west | Av. Albert 1er)* in the *museum (mid-May–mid-Sep Tue–Sun 9.30am–1pm, 2.30pm–6.30pm, otherwise 10am–1.30pm, 2.30pm–5pm | 6 euros | Rue Capouane | www.trophee-auguste.fr).*

NICE AND SURROUNDS

There can only ever be one true star to play the lead role, and on the French Riviera it's clearly Nice! With its gently curved 10 km/6.2 mi long beach, its Promenade des Anglais, its belle époque palaces, picturesque houses, baroque art treasures, its museums and hints of Italy it continues to attract streams of visitors.

Despite their proximity to Nice, towns like Saint-Jean-Cap-Ferrat or Villefranche-sur-Mer have managed to retain their own unique character, and out of season they are relaxed. A few miles north is where the mountainous region begins, with lots of small villages precariously clinging to the hill tops. The French call them *villages perchés* or perched villages. The houses are interlaced and nestled snugly against

one another and the villages all full of steep, narrow and vaulted alleyways.

NICE

MAP INSIDE BACK COVER
(141 E–F 2–3) (*O–P 6–7*) You can really let it all hang out in Nice: enjoy a chic cocktail wearing a jogging suit. Enjoy a cool swim on the beach promenade in the morning, and in the afternoon take the bus to the skiing region. Drink toxic green absinthe in the old town until the ochre-coloured buildings start to sway before your eyes. Dance the salsa in the moonlight at midnight as you enjoy a violet and chestnut ice cream.

Photo: Promenade des Anglais in Nice

The towns along the French Riviera coast are strung along like pearls with Nice as its glittering jewel

CITY WHERE TO START?
Place Masséna: Old town Nice and the Promenade des Anglais are within easy walking distance from Place Masséna. The square was converted into a pedestrian precinct with the launch of a tram system. By the way – the *Saleya* car park is an alternative if the *Masséna* car park is full.

The capital of the Départements Alpes-Maritimes (pop. 350,000) is not quite as sophisticated as Cannes, but it's lively and popular on 365 days of the year thanks to student and working-class districts such as *Riquier* on the harbour. The best thing is to head into one of the pubs around 6 pm and share a pastis with the French at the end of the working day. Listening to old chansons and eating garlic-soaked olives with their fingers.

Above all, though, Nice is famous for its 7 km/4.4 mi beach promenade, the

41

Shop, restaurant, shop, restaurant... there's endless shopping and dining in Nice's old town

⭐ *Promenade des Anglais* that was originally financed by the British. Which is why the locals were even more horrified when a terrorist drove a lorry into 86 people here in the summer of 2016. After numerous memorial services and a year-long halt to events, they have now reconquered their promenade. Joggers, inline skaters and cyclists compete against each other, past the loveliest hotel in the region, the snow-white *Négresco* with liveried staff and a sparkling golden entrance hall. The five-star establishment is wickedly expensive, but everyone should sip champagne on its terrace at least once in their lifetime! A few feet further along is where the new **INSIDER TIP** *Promenade du Paillon* starts: the lovely park with play areas, fountains and impressively tall palm trees is so popular with families that children actually queue for the slides. Right next to it are the crooked streets of the *old town*. Even at the height of summer it's pleasantly cool here, and the air is full of the wonderful smells of hand-made leather bags, soaps and spic-

es. The ochre and rust-red houses are reminders of Nice's Italian history: the city became part of France as the result of a referendum in 1860. Since then "Nissa la Bella" – Nice the Lovely – has attracted wealthy, sun-loving people from all over the world. Even Russian nobility fled from their icy winters to warm Nice, leaving the cathedral of *Saint-Nicolas (Av. Nicolas II)* that was inaugurated by the Tsar's family in 1912, which is not far from the main station. The colourful onion towers are very pretty, but be aware if you attend a service: the faithful stand – for all of two hours.

Take the tram *to Place Garibaldi* to the north of the old town. The historic façades glow golden in the evenings, while during the day you can enjoy a *café au lait* under the pink blossom of the silk trees. The city is currently building a second tramway that starts underground at the harbour and is to run parallel to the sea promenade to the airport. Those who wish to explore the loveliest parts of Nice that are only open to pedestrians should take advantage of one of the many INSIDER TIP rickshaws waiting on Masséna Square. They are usually ridden by friendly students, who enjoy telling you all sorts of personal things about their city.

SIGHTSEEING

VIEILLE VILLE

Old town Nice has been extensively restored and its alleyways and squares, colourful houses, hustle and bustle of its markets, restaurants and shops make it absolutely charming. The most impressive piece of architecture may well be the hardest to find. In a narrow alleyway, the museum INSIDER TIP *Palais Lascaris* (Tue–Mon 10am–6pm | 15, Rue Droite) dates back to the 17th century and has an unusual façade, a massive staircase and a distinctive Genoese style. Other baroque masterpieces are the *Sainte-Réparate* cathedral on Place Rosetti, *Chapelle de la Miséricorde* on Cours Saleya and *Église Saint-Jacques* (also called *Église du Gesù*) in the Rue Droite. Three squares give the old town its architectural style; *Place Garibaldi* – with its statue of the freedom fighter – is surrounded by arcades, *Place Saint-François* with the town hall and fish market and *Cours Saleya* in the south with the colourful flower market. It's also the tastiest spot of all: enjoy candied fruit and fresh oranges on the market in the morning, an inexpensive three-course menu on the terraces at lunchtime, and then in the evening down a pastis with students and tourists from all over the world.

BUTTE DU CHÂTEAU

Three hundred years ago, the entire village of Nice lived on this hill. Today, you can see as far as the airport and the 3000-m/10,000-ft peaks of the hinterland from the lookout points.
And be sure to take a photo at the *Cascade d'Amour* – the Waterfall of Love! – with dripping wet hair.

⭐ **Promenade des Anglais**
The English financed this promenade lined with palm trees and palatial buildings → p. 42

⭐ **Musée National Marc Chagall**
The largest collection of the artist's work is housed in Nice → p. 44

⭐ **Markets**
A feast for the senses in old town Nice – flowers, fresh produce, fish and meat → p. 46

⭐ **Musée National Fernand Léger**
An artist's legacy of giant ceramics and powerful paintings in Biot → p. 48

⭐ **Cap Ferrat**
On the peninsula of monarchs and millionaires – palatial villas, glorious gardens and small beaches → p. 49

⭐ **Eze**
A showcase *village perché* high above the sea – even Nietzsche has holidayed here → p. 50

⭐ **Chapelle du Rosaire**
Artist and designer in one – Matisse's chapel in Vence → p. 52

⭐ **Fondation Maeght**
Superb private art museum in Saint-Paul-de-Vence → p. 53

MARCO POLO HIGHLIGHTS

MARCHÉ DE LA LIBÉRATION

Yes, we know – the Cours Saleya is right by the sea and also sells bags of lavender to tourists. But if you want to see real farmers and shouting fishmongers, take the tram to Libération. For the city's most local fruit and vegetables! *Tue–Fri 6am–12.30pm | Place du Général de Gaulle*

MUSÉE D'ART MODERNE ET D'ART CONTEMPORAIN (MAMAC)

"The creation of doubt" is a quote by Ben. Or: "We must mistrust words". Nice's best-known artist is, of all things, someone who doesn't want to be one. Like Andy Warhol, Ben wants to declare everyday life as art. His quotes, written in a child's handwriting in white on a black background, can be seen at the tram stops – and in the biggest modern museum in Nice, the MAMAC. The museum's pride and joy are works by Nice-born Yves Klein (1928–62) among them some of his famous **INSIDER TIP** Blue Epoch pictures donated to the museum by Niki de Saint-Phalle. Art lovers will find also works by Andy Warhol, Rob Rauschenberg and Tom Wesselmann. Its 🔆 roof top patio has a spectacular view over the city and the sea. *Tue–Sun 10am–6pm | 10 euros | Place Yves Klein | www.mamac-nice.org*

MUSÉE MATISSE ●

Henri Matisse (1869–1954) resided in Nice from 1917 until his death, and this 17th century Genoese villa in an olive grove in Cimiez has a large collection of his work and displays his artistic beginnings through to his last work. *Wed–Mon 10am–6pm | 10 euros | 164, Av. des Arènes de Cimiez | bus Arènes/Musée Matisse | www.musee-matisse-nice.org*

MUSÉE NATIONAL MARC CHAGALL ★

Cimiez is home to a purpose built museum with the most comprehensive collection of Marc Chagall's (1887–1985) works. Its focus is the biblical messages contained in his paintings, sculptures

Competition for the beach: water fun in the lovely new park at the Promenade du Paillon

and tapestries, as well as mosaics of the Prophet Elijah on the building's façade. *May–Oct Wed–Mon 10am–6pm, Nov–April 10am–5pm | 8 euros | Av. du Docteur Ménard | bus Musée Chagall | www.musee-chagall.fr*

PROMENADE DU PAILLON ●

A bright idea by the mayor of Nice, of all things a former racing driver: get rid of the streets and underground garages, let the palm and olive trees and grass grow – and you have the perfect city garden. Dangle your feet in the water fountains in summer.

INSIDER TIP ▶ VILLA ARSON

This beautiful 18th century villa estate with its modern Bauhaus extension is a modern art academy. The academy puts on some of the most exciting exhibitions on the Mediterranean art circuit. *Wed–Mon 2pm–6pm | entrance free | Av. Stephen Liégard | bus Le Ray or Deux Avenues | www.villa-arson.org*

LE BISTROT D'ANTOINE

You shudder at the sight of black pudding and have never tried liver stew? Then get yourself to the *Bistrot d'Antoine*! You'll survive the culinary test of courage – and be proud of yourself: the traditional "poor people's" food served at this bistro in the old town is good enough to serve a king. Wood tables, checked tablecloths and a wrought iron bar are just how we imagine French restaurants to be. Be sure to book! *Closed Sun/Mon | 27, Rue de la Préfecture | tel. 04 93 85 29 57 | Moderate*

LE CAFÉ DE TURIN

Two restaurants that serve excellent seafood in the arcades of Place Garibaldi are *Turin (Tue–Thu)* and *Turinissimo (closed Sun evenings and for lunch on Mon/Tue)* but if a plate of freshly prepared oysters is what you are after, then Le Grand Café is for you – established in 1908 it is an institution in Nice. *Daily | 5, Place Garibaldi | tel. 04 93 62 29 52 | www.cafedeturin.fr | Budget–Expensive*

COMPTOIR CENTRAL ELECTRIQUE

This quarter in the north of the old town between the Place Garibaldi and the harbour is becoming the new gastro meeting place in Nice. The vintage bistro is housed within a former electrical shop with the original decorations, terrace and creative cuisine. *Closed Sun | 10, Rue Bonaparte | tel. 04 93 14 09 62 | FB/lecomptoircentralelectrique | Budget–Moderate*

LA MERENDA

Superb local specialities served by chef Le Stanc who only uses fresh market produce. The restaurant is tiny, so may not be ideal for a confidential tête-à-tête. *Closed Sat/Sun, reservations essential | 4, Rue Raoul Bosio | Budget–Moderate*

INSIDERTIP **L'UNION** ●

Tourists rarely stray to the burgeoning Borriglione quarter, where Daniel Alvarez has his brasserie with a summer garden and petanque pitch, and serves specialities from Nice such as *pissaladière, tripes, beignets* and *daube du boeuf* at sensible prices. *Daily | 1, Rue Michelet | tel. 04 93 84 65 27 | tramway Valrose-Université | www.unionrestaurant.fr | Budget*

SHOPPING

For olive oil, head to **INSIDERTIP** Nicolas Alziari *(14, Rue Saint-François de Paule)*. Candied fruit, bars of chocolate and chocolate are available from *Maison Auer (7, Rue Saint-François de Paule)*. Browse the small antiques market *Les Puces de Nice (Tue–Sat 10am–6pm)* in the harbour. If you're looking for fashion, head for the streets around the Rue de la Liberté. You'll find the major brands in the quarter to the west of Avenue Jean Médecin between Boulevard Victor Hugo and Promenade des Anglais. For 100 boutiques under one roof, go to ● *Nicetoile (30, Av. Jean Médecin | www.nicetoile.com)*.

MARKETS ★

The *fish market (Tue–Sun 6am–1pm)* on the Place Saint-François is legendary for its fabulous offer. A few steps further, the *Cours Saleya*, home to the *Marché aux fleurs (Tue–Sat 6am–5.30pm, Sun 6am–noon)*, has more flowers than you can imagine. There's also the equally colourful *food market (Tue–Sun 7am–1pm)*.

SPORTS & BEACHES

Sun worshippers have a choice of 20 public beaches (another 15 are private) along a 7 km/4.4 mi stretch. On Plage *Opéra-Beau Rivage* you can hire waterskiing, paragliding, canoeing and kayaking equipment from *Nikaia Water Sports (www.nikaiaglisse.com)* and for those on a bicycle or scooter, the *Promenade des Anglais* has a dedicated lane. Nice has many spa options e. g. *Deep Nature spa (Hotel Boscolo Exedra | 12, Blvd. Victor Hugo | www.deepnature.fr)* and the spa at *Hôtel Splendid (50, Blvd. Victor Hugo | www.spa-splendid.com)* which also caters for day visitors, but its rooftop ☆ pool is exclusively for hotel guests.

SKIING ●

Skiing on the French Riviera? Is that true? Yes, it's true. So true, in fact, that lots of schools head for the white pistes of the Maritime Alps on their Wednesdays off. Between November and April, the *Snow bus* will take you from the bus station in Nice to smaller ski resorts such as Valberg and Auron, and the bigger, somewhat crowded Isola 2000. And even if you get the last bus back, there will still be time for a cocktail on the beach. Honestly! *www.cotedazur-neige.com*

ENTERTAINMENT

Fritter away your money in the casinos, drink cocktails in lively bars or simply take a bottle of red wine down to the beach with you – you can do any (or all) of that in Nice! The meeting place is the old town around the *Cours Saleya* with live bands at *Wayne's (15, Rue de la Préfecture | www.waynes.fr)*. Nightly DJs at the *Happy Bar* of the *Hi Hôtel (38 rooms | 3, Av. des Fleurs | tel. 04 97 07 26 26 | www.hi-hotel.net)* with ❂ organic restaurant *(Expensive)*.

INSIDERTIP **COURT-CIRCUIT CAFÉ** ❂

Careful, careful – put your poker face on, please! No tourists have yet been sighted at the "Court-circuit". No one who comes to this café – or is it a bar? a club? – has any idea what to expect. You might dance a tango, hear the latest punk bands from Nice, or eat cake as you listen to fairytales. Also available: organic food from local farmers, home-brewed beer and all-night conversations

04 93 16 64 00 | www.hotel-negresco-nice.com | *Expensive*

LE PETIT LOUVRE

A simple but charming, reasonably priced establishment with small rooms for young tourists. Friendly staff.

Vegetable variety at the Cours Saleya. How to keep perspective? Oh, with commitment and earnestness

with young people who want to change the world. *Tue–Thu 9am–10pm, Fri/Sat until midnight, Sun 11.30am–4pm | 4, Rue Vernier | behind the station | tel. 09 82 31 65 33 | www.courtcircuitcafe.org*

WHERE TO STAY

NÉGRESCO ●

This iconic deluxe hotel with its façades, spectacular glass dome and Baccarat chandelier offers exquisite belle époque style elegance and was officially declared a national monument.

It also houses the top restaurant *Le Chantecler (Closed on Mon/Tue and in Jan | Expensive)*, the brasserie *La Rotonde (Moderate–Expensive)* and the bar *Le Relais (11.30am–1pm)* with its updated 1913 décor. *117 rooms and suites | 37, Promenade des Anglais | tel.*

31 rooms | Closed Nov–Jan | 10, Rue Emma et Philippe Tiranty | tel. 04 93 80 15 54 | www.hotelpetitlouvre.fr | Budget

INSIDER TIP HÔTEL WINDSOR

In the middle of the city, but with a garden, pool and wellness area. Almost every year there is a new surprise in art. Like the entrance hall, most of the rooms and the restaurant were designed by artists such as Ben, Lawrence Weiner, François Morellet and Gottfried Honegger. *57 rooms | 11, Rue Dalpazzo | tel. 04 93 88 59 35 | www.hotelwindsornice.com | Expensive*

INFORMATION

Tourist information is available at the train station *(Av. Thiers)* or in the city centre *(5, Promenade des Anglais | tel.*

08 92 70 74 07 | www.nicetourisme.com). The *French Riviera Pass (26 euros for 1 day, 38 euros for 2 days)* includes a grand city tour, as well as guided tours and discounts.

WHERE TO GO

BEAULIEU-SUR-MER (141 F3) *(⌕ P7)*
A typical example of a beautiful belle époque seaside resort with its palms and palatial villas. Master builder Gustave Eiffel once lived here. It is the start of a coastal path that even the most fragile tourist can manage with ease. Past the *Villa Grecque Kérylos (Feb–June, Sept–Oct daily 10am–6pm, July/Aug 10am–7pm, Nov–Feb Mon–Fri 2pm–6pm, Sat/Sun 10am–6pm | 11.50 euros | www.villakerylos.com)*, which is based on a copy of a classic Greek villa: the severe lines are not particularly exciting, but it's pretty to look at.

BIOT ● (141 D4) *(⌕ N–O7)*
Pottery craft dates back to antiquity in Biot (population of 9000) 20 km/12.4 mi west of Nice and today the picturesque town is also renowned for its glass and jewellery artists. Watch the glass-blowers at work: La *Verrerie de Biot (summer Mon–Sat 9.30am–8pm, Sun 10am–1pm, 3pm–7pm, winter Mon–Sat 9.30am–6pm, Sun 10.30am–1pm, 2.30pm–6.30pm | Chemin des Combes | www.verreriebiot.com).*

The town has been linked to artist Fernand Léger (1881–1955) since 1960 when his widow donated 348 of his works which are now housed in the ★ *Musée National Fernand Léger (Wed–Mon 10am–5pm, May–Oct until 6pm | 5.50 euros | Chemin du Val de Pome | www.musees-nationaux-alpesmaritimes.fr/fleger).* A 5380 ft^2 mosaic forms the façade of the building and reflects his signature style of heavily outlined colour fields.

Proprietors Mimi and André Brothier of hotel's on-site restaurant *les Arcades (restaurant Sun evening, closed Mon | 16, Place des Arcades | tel. 04 93 65 01 04 | www.hotel-restaurant-les-arcades.com | Restaurant Budget–Moderate | hotel with 12 rooms, Budget–Moderate)* have been collecting INSIDER TIP artworks by artists like Fernand Léger and Victor Vasarely for more than 40 years and display them in their vaulted cellar. The restaurant's Provençal cuisine may be a little expensive but the hotel rooms are beautifully decorated. Information: *46, Rue Saint-Sébastien | tel. 04 93 65 78 00 | www.biot-tourisme.com*

CAGNES-SUR-MER (141 D–E3) *(⌕ O7)*
Close your eyes and go for it: if you want to get from the beach to the old town of Cagnes-sur-Mer (pop. 49,000; 15 km/9.3 mi west), you mustn't mind

Bathe and dream of the luxury properties to the left and right: Paloma Beach at Cap Ferrat

the traffic and the hum of the motorway too much. Because as soon as you get to the ☙ old town, the quiet streets and lovely views of the sea beyond these smellies will calm you down again. Take a stroll through the alleyways beneath the medieval castle and you will see why so many artists called this village home. Pierre-Auguste Renoir (1841–1919) had a house in the middle of *Les Collettes* olive grove. Completely refurbished in 2013, this building with the lovely garden and bronze sculpture *Venus Victrix* is today the *Musée Renoir (summer Wed–Mon 10am–noon, 2pm–6pm, in winter until 5pm | 6 euros)* and both memorial and museum. As a contrast, you can shop till you drop – at Cagnes' *Polygone Riviera (Mon–Sat 10am–9pm, Sun 11am–7pm)* there are 150 shops waiting for you. It claims to be the first open-air shopping centre, and soon, when the almost 1000 trees that have been planted there, have grown it'll be like shopping in a forest ... Information: *Office de Tourisme (6, Blvd. Maréchal Juin | Cagnes-sur-Mer | tel. 04 93 20 61 64 | www.cagnes-tourisme.com)*

CAP FERRAT ★ (141 F3) (*ℳ P7*)

You'll see better in the dark: if you want to understand the unimaginable wealth of the millionaires' peninsula at the old fishing village of *Saint-Jean-Cap-Ferrat* (pop. 2100, 6 km/3.7 mi to the east), you'd best come in the middle of the night, when you'll be able to see the sparkling chandeliers inside the villas and the liveried staff at the tall entrances. By day, it's better to take the coastal trail (*sentier littoral*), which will take you once around the peninsula in about two hours. The loveliest estate on the Cap with fabulous views of the house and garden is open to visitors: In 1910 the baroness Béatrice Ephnussi de Rothschild built ● *Villa Ephrussi de Rothschild (Feb–Oct daily 10am–6pm, July/Aug until 7pm, Nov–Jan 2pm–6pm | 14 euros | www.villa-ephrussi.com)*, an Italianate palazzo. Together

Can cacti be happy? The ones at the *Jardin Exotique* are sure to be, because they have a sea view

with a 17-acre park it forms the *Musée Île-de-France* with more than 5000 artworks on exhibit. Information: *5 and 59, Av. Denis Séméria 29 | tel. 04 93 76 08 90 | www.saintjeancapferrat-tourisme.fr*

EZE ★ ⚘ (141 F2) (*ω P6*)

Clinging to the cliff 427 m/1401 ft vertically above the sea, this village is said to have been named after the Egyptian goddess Isis. With a population of around 3000, Eze is 10 km/6.2 mi east of Nice and is a typical example of a *village perché*. Stroll through the restored stone village with its steep alleyways and you will see why the philosopher Nietzsche chose to live here. If you decide to take the path from the coastal town of *Eze-Bord-de-Mer* up to the mountain it will take about two hours (there and back) and you will need to be very fit.

Eze is known for its *Jardin Exotique (summer 9am–8pm, otherwise 9am–5.30pm | 6 euros)* on top of the hill in the grounds of a ruined 14th century castle. Enjoy spectacular views of the Riviera from its terraces. Loïc Siino has opened his own restaurant in the village, *L'Alchimie (closed Sun| 197, Av. de Verdun | tel. 04 93 41 12 79 | www.restaurant-lalchimie. com | Moderate–Expensive)*, which serves fabulous creations. Information: *Place de Gaulle | tel. 04 93 41 26 00 | www.eze-tourisme.com*

INSIDER TIP LUCÉRAM ●
(141 F1) (*ω P5*)

A name that will set any cyclist's pulse racing: Lucéram (pop. 1200), 25 km/15.5 mi north of Nice, is en route to the legendary Turini Pass and, as you would expect, the road winds its way through the village around tight bends. History is evident wherever you go in the abundance of treasures. The *Église Sainte-Marguerite* has altarpieces by Giovanni Canavesio and Louis Bréa representing some of the most remarkable baroque works of *l'École de Nice*. Christmas Eve is celebrated with a traditional nativity procession to the church and it joins the village *Piera-Cava* (14 km/8.7 mi north) from Dec–Jan with INSIDER TIP *450 circuit des crèches*, private nativity scenes set up in the narrow village streets. Information: *6, Place Adrien Barralis | tel. 04 93 79 91 60 | www.luceram.com*

PEILLON (137 D5) (*ᨓ P6*)

Peillon (pop. 130) is the village without streets: the houses in the old town are built so steeply into the mountain that the only way to get up and down the alleys is on foot. Little wonder, then, that one of the loveliest climbing trails starts at this eyrie. The best time to go is in the morning, because the sun is unbelievably strong at midday! If you prefer a quieter life, drive – or take the lovely trail – to neighbouring ⊰ᨓ *Peille* (pop. 2200). Lovely views, but no café.

VILLEFRANCHE-SUR-MER
(141 F3) (*ᨓ P7*)

A charming coastal town (population of 6600) beneath the historic 16th century *La Citadelle* built by the Duke of Sa-

voy which is a museum *(Oct–May daily 10am–noon, 3pm–5.30pm, Jun–Sep daily 10am–noon, 3pm–6.30pm, closed Sun morning | free entrance)* that houses sculptures by Antoniucci Volti and the valuable collection of artist couple Christine Boumeester and Henri Goetz.

Jean Cocteau decorated the *Chapelle Saint-Pierre* in 1957 *(Wed–Mon 10am–noon, 3pm–7pm (summer), 2pm–6pm (winter), closed mid Nov–mid Dec | 3 euros)*. Information: *Jardin François Binon | tel. 04 93 01 73 68 | www.villefranche-sur-mer.com*

VENCE

(141 D2) (*ᨓ O6*) **Wow, this really is an all-year place. And that's a compliment on the French Riviera, because Vence (pop. 19,000) is alive all year round, and its market square with the wonderful plane trees is well worth a visit.**
The town is as romantic as a village in the Provence, but as lively as the French Riviera. There are walking trails

FOR BOOKWORMS AND FILM BUFFS

Ducasse: Flavours of France – Possibly not ideal for cooking yourself, but a fabulous read: the thick book by Monaco's star chef Alain Ducasse. After reading it, you'll understand why a starter at Ducasse can cost 40 euros

Tender is the Night – Generally regarded to be F. Scott Fitzgerald's most important novel. It is set in a small Riviera coastal town in the 1930s and portrays a set of characters that are beautiful, wealthy, sophisticated and idle

The Transporter – In this French action film (2002), Frank (Jason Statham) is living a quiet life in Fréjus – while at the same time „working" as a petty criminal all along the French Riviera. Brisk action, plenty of flair

To Catch a Thief – Eze, Monaco, Cagnes-sur-Mer, the Route de la Grande Corniche and Nice: the French Riviera is the real star of Alfred Hitchcock's 1955 classic – starring Grace Kelly and Cary Grant

to the *Col de Vence*, a pass that looks as if it were in an extinct moon landscape.

SIGHTSEEING

OLD TOWN

They all come to Vence: the hikers who rest against the medieval town walls, the cyclists who refresh themselves at one of the three fountains on the *Place du Peyra*, and the tourists who browse the pretty little shops. The museum *Château de Villeneuve,* once the bastion of the rulers of Vence on the Place du Frêne, also has a 500 year old ash tree *(Château de Villeneuve | Fondation Emile Hugues | Tue–Sun 10am–12.30pm, 2pm–6pm, July/Aug 10am–6pm | 7 euros)*. It also holds contemporary art exhibitions.

Its *Saint-Véran* cathedral has an 11th century nave, 15th century choir stalls and a 19th century façade as well as a stunning Marc Chagall mosaic in its baptistery. The mosaic depicts Moses being rescued from the Nile.

CHAPELLE DU ROSAIRE ★

Henri Matisse designed this Dominican chapel a few minutes walk outside Vence on the road leading to the impressive *Baou de Saint-Jeannet* mountain summit. *Mon, Wed, Sat 2pm–5.30pm, Fri (only during the holiday period) 2pm–5.30pm, Tue/Thu 10am–11.30am and 2pm–5.30pm. Sun for mass at 10am, closed mid Nov–mid Dec | 6 euros | 446, Av. Henri Matisse*

FOOD & DRINK

AUBERGE DES SEIGNEURS

Is a traditional hotel and restaurant in a 17th century building centrally located in old town Vence near the castle. All of the six rooms *(Moderate)* are named after famous painters. *Closed Sun/Mon | 1, Rue du Dr Binet | tel. 04 93 58 04 24 | www. auberge-seigneurs.com | Moderate*

CHOCOLAT PARBONA

This place – or what it sells – will go straight to your hips! In Patrice's shop, you can admire the machines that make the wonderful chocolates, and enjoy the matching hot chocolate at the counter. Wonderful! Just forget your good intentions, just this once – it's worth it. *Closed 1pm–3pm and Sun | 12, Av. Marcellin Maurel*

SHOPPING

Vence is a centre for arts and crafts and has some exquisite galleries and appealing markets *(Tue–Sun every morning on the squares: Grand-Jardin and Place Surian).*

WHERE TO STAY

LA LUBIANE

An unpretentious small hotel on the banks of the Lubiane river about 400 m from the city centre. It has a patio full of flowers and an affordable restaurant *(Budget)*. *14 rooms | closed 15 Nov–Jan | 10, Av. Maréchal Joffre | tel. 04 93 58 01 10 | www.lubiane.fr | Budget*

VILLA ROSERAIE ☙

Art nouveau villa with swimming pool, patio and garden 400 m/1312 ft from the city centre. *9 rooms | closed mid Nov–mid Feb | 128, Av. Henri Giraud | tel. 04 93 58 02 20 | www.villaroseraie.com | Moderate–Expensive*

INFORMATION

Place du Grand Jardin | tel. 04 93 58 06 38 | www.vence.fr

SAINT-PAUL-DE-VENCE ●
(141 D3) (*M Q7*)

This pretty little town has already turned unsuspecting people into artists. So wait and see what happens on the INSIDER TIP accessible town wall and in the narrow alleys. With a population of 3300 now it is considered to be one of the most exclusive spots in the entire French Riviera. It is also home to the legendary restaurant *La Colombe d'Or (daily | Place du Général de Gaulle | tel. 04 93 32 80 02 | www.la-colombe-dor.com | Expensive | also 25 rooms | with a swimming pool and gardens | Expensive)*. Pablo Picasso and Georges Braque are only some of the big names in modern art to leave the restaurant some of their works. Marc Chagall also spent nearly 20 years here. Perfectly located at the village entrance is *Café de la Place (1, Place du Général de Gaulle | tel. 04 93 32 80 03 | Budget)* at the big boules square. Information: *2, Rue Grande | tel. 04 93 32 86 95 | www.saint-pauldevence.com*

Just outside Saint-Paul-de-Vence is the remarkable ★ *Fondation Maeght (daily 10am–6pm, in midsummer until 7pm | 15 euros | www.fondation-maeght.com)* (pronounced: ma-h-g) one of the most beautiful private museums in the world and a major draw card for art lovers since 1964. Catalan architect Josep Lluis Sert together with artists like Joan Miró, Georges Braque, Alberto Giacometti and Marc Chagall designed the light-coloured concrete and red brick building for the collector couple Aimé and Marguerite Maeght. It fits harmoniously into the Mediterranean landscape. There are huge sculptures outdoors and the building itself houses large collections of modern art and new temporary exhibits change annually.

Perfect aid to the digestion: walk once around the town wall of Saint-Paul-de-Vence

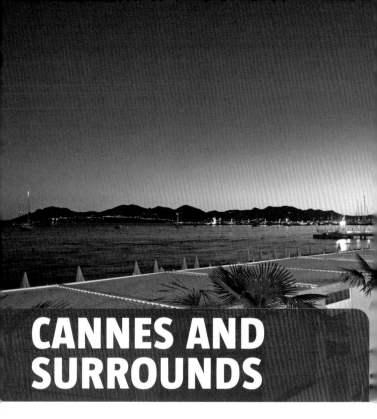

CANNES AND SURROUNDS

Please leave your hiking sandals in your suitcase. In Cannes, your LBD will also be perfect at lunchtime, and a suit and highly polished shoes are anyway. It's simply not possible to be over-dressed here.

The glamorous home of the film festival is worth a visit just for star-watching. And the old town is such a delight that you'll feel you could slip back into your old sandals. In contrast the tranquil hinterland provides Grasse with the wonderful fragrances that it needs for its perfumes.

ANTIBES

(141 D4) (*Ø O8*) **Antibes (pop. 74,000) is so delightful that everyone checks the** property prices first to see if they can't possibly afford a tiny apartment in the old town. But forget it: the city is considered one of the most expensive in France. The stone houses in the old town are surrounded by wine, plus there's a world-class Picasso museum and sand beaches for surfing on the Cap d'Antibes – simply brilliant.

SIGHTSEEING

OLD TOWN

Parts of the fortification walls or *remparts*, which once protected *Vieil Antibes* from attacks from Nice, are still intact. For centuries *Porte Marine* was the only access to the harbour. Slightly further on is *Place du Révèly* with its *Chapelle du*

At the home of the Golden Palms: Cannes and Antibes are classic lidos, while Grasse provides lovely fragrances

Saint-Esprit and *Cathédrale* and the *Château Grimaldi* in all its glory where the Picasso Museum is housed today. Another attraction is the *covered marketplace* Marché Provençal on *Cours Masséna*. The narrow *Rue du Bas-Castelet* with its picturesque houses adorned with flowers takes you to *Safranier*, a free state within the city that has had its own mayor since 1966. From the fortress tower *Bastion Saint-André* it is easy to find your way back to *La Gravette* a wind protected beach in the old harbour.

CAP D'ANTIBES ★

Here luxury mansions with fantastic gardens can be seen alongside ordinary holiday homes. Follow the pilgrim route (*Chemin du Calvaire*) and walk up to the *Chapelle de la Garoupe (daily 9.30am–noon, 2.30pm–7pm, in winter open until 5pm)* and then go on to the lighthouse ⚡ *Phare de la Garoupe* which has superb views from its platform.

Tucked away in the middle of the peninsula is the 9-acre *Jardin Thuret*. Here Gustave Thuret planted the French Riviera's

Not just a pretty postcard: the fishmermen still bring their catches into the harbour of Antibes every day

first palms and eucalyptus trees in 1857 *(Mon–Fri 8am–6pm, in winter 8.30am–5.30pm | free entrance)*. A coastal hiking trail leads around the gardens all the way to *Villa Eilenroc (Sept–June Tue, Wed, Sat 9am–5pm | free entrance)* with a nice park, which Charles Garnier designed in 1867 for its rich Dutch owner. Today the villa typifies the unique charm the cape is trying to uphold in the face of extensive development.

MUSÉE PICASSO ★

The man in the striped T-shirt with the countless lovers and thousands of paintings is the star of Antibes: Picasso opened a studio in the city in 1945, and today he is honoured in the former *Grimaldi Palace*, by a fabulous museum. Be sure to treat yourself to a little Piccolo at sundown and raise it on the terrace, by the fabulous sculptures by Germaine Richter and Anne and Patrick Poirier that are standing there, to the sea view and to life. Inside the building, the **INSIDER TIP** hall dedicated to Nicolas de Staël is a delight and its art by Alexander Calder, Fernand Léger, Amadeo Modigliani, Max Ernst and Hans Hartung makes it a prestigious art venue on the French Riviera. *Daily 10am–noon, 2pm–6pm, in summer Tue–Sun 10am–6pm, July/Aug Wed and Fri until 8pm | 6 euros | Place Mariejol*

FOOD & DRINK

INSIDER TIP ARTS THÉS MISS ☺

For the hip and the idealists: the food served at this cute restaurant in the old town is organic, fresh, vegan, lactose- and gluten-free. *Daily in summer 9am–4pm, Fri 6pm–11pm, shorter opening times in winter (see website) | 19, Rue de*

Rennes | reservations via SMS 06 63 42 85 24 | artsthesmiss.com | *Moderate*

LE DISTROT DU CURÉ

You don't have to expect bread and water at the "Curate's Bistro". It's simple, but also simply delicious: cheeses, onion cake, fruit salad, all enjoyed under the shade of the plane trees next door to the church. *Daily in summer 10am–8.30pm, from mid-Sept Tue-Sun 11.30am–6pm | Plateau de La Garoupe/Route du Phare | at Cap d'Antibes | tel. 04 93 61 35 87 | le bistrotducure.fr | Budget*

BEACHES & LEISURE

Cap d'Antibes is known for its beautiful bays and the most sought after beaches are in Juan-les-Pins. The *Institut Thalazur (770, chemin des Moyennes Bréguières | tel. 04 92 91 82 02 | www. thalazur.fr)* in Antibes is one of the most renowned centres for thalassotherapy on the French Riviera and also offers ⊕ organic cosmetic treatments.

ENTERTAINMENT

There are lots of cafés and bars in Antibes and Juan-les-Pins that stay open till late in summer. One of the biggest entertainment spots is *La Siesta (summer daily 10am–4pm | 2000, Route du bord de mer | direction of Nice)* with a casino and several dance floors.

WHERE TO STAY

LA BASTIDE DU BOSQUET

Stay in an 18th century villa where author Guy de Maupassant also spent his holidays. *4 rooms | 14, Chemin des Sables | tel. 06 51 76 72 73 | rooms from May-mid Oct, at all other times the house is let by the week | www.lebosquet06.com | Expensive*

LA JABOTTE

A beautifully decorated establishment only 60 m/196.9 ft from Cap d'Antibes' Salis beach. *10 rooms | 13, Av. Max Maurey | tel. 04 93 61 45 89 | www.jabotte. com | Moderate–Expensive*

LE RELAIS DU POSTILLON

Near the pedestrian zone of old town Antibes, its rooms are small but pristine. *16 rooms | 8, Rue Championnet | tel. 04 93 34 20 77 | www.relaisdupostillon.com | Moderate*

INFORMATION

11, Place de Gaulle | tel. 04 92 90 53 00 | www.antibesjuanlespins.com

MARCO POLO HIGHLIGHTS

⭐ **Cap d'Antibes**
Lush peninsula with palatial houses and botanical garden
→ **p. 55**

⭐ **Musée Picasso**
In Antibes – paintings, sculptures and ceramics → **p. 56**

⭐ **Boulevard de la Croisette**
Cannes version of the Promenade des Anglais in Nice → **p. 58**

⭐ **Iles de Lérins**
Liqueurs and an archaeological treasure trove on the islands off Cannes → **p. 61**

⭐ **Vallauris-Golfe-Juan**
Picasso's "Man with a sheep" and many of his other works → **p. 62**

⭐ **Grasse**
Awaken the senses in the world's perfume capital → **p. 62**

CANNES

WHERE TO GO

JUAN-LES-PINS (141 D4) (*𝄞 O8*)
THE place for people who want to swim and fry in the sun. Sandy beaches, bikini stalls and cocktails at Happy Hour guaranteed. Before World War II it was the playground for rich Americans who brought jazz to Europe and after 1945 it became the centre for swing. Since 1959 the *Pinède Gould* summer jazz festival has been held here. Information: *51, Blvd. Charles Guillaumont | tel. 04 97 23 11 10 | www.antibesjuanlespins.com*

CANNES

 **MAP INSIDE BACK COVER**
(140–141 C–D 4–5) (*𝄞 N8*)
Perhaps the city with the most important carpet in the world: every year, the 150-m/492-ft long red runner welcomes half of Hollywood as well as stars from Berlin and Paris to the annual film festival.

Apart from the chunky festival building, the city (pop. 73,000) also has an amazingly attractive old town, and the boat rides out to the islands off the coast will help you to forget the – occasionally undeniably tiring – glamour.

> 🏙 **WHERE TO START?**
> **Boulevard de la Croisette:** the boulevard along the Mediterranean coast is an ideal starting point from which to explore Cannes, be it the old town Le Suquet district or the festival palace. Parking is a rare commodity in the city centre so best to leave your car at the **Parc du Palais** *(1, Blvd. de la Croisette, max. height 1.80 m/5.9 ft!)* parkade.

SIGHTSEEING

BOULEVARD DE LA CROISETTE ⭐
There's no such thing as "too much" when it comes to outfits for the ladies on the lovely Croisette: you won't find higher heels anywhere else. La Croisette is the counterpart to Nice's Promenade des Anglais and also has palm trees, palatial buildings, exclusive boutiques and sandy beaches along an inviting bay. At the western end lies, off the harbour, the famous *Palais des Festivals et des Congrès*, a concrete building inaugurated in 1983, which not only hosts the *Festival du Cannes* in May, but is also host to trade fairs such as Midem (music) and Mip-tv (television) all year round.
The handprints of at least 200 movie stars have been eternalised in the paving of the *Allée des Stars*. Also worth a closer look are the façades of the *Majestic, Carlton* and *Martinez* hotels.

LE SUQUET
Cannes' historic old town centre at the foot of Mont Chevalier is a small maze of about ten streets, one of them is Rue Saint-Antoine which winds its way up to the fort where the archaeological collection of the monks of the Iles de Lérins is housed. *Musée de la Castre (Sept–May Tue–Sun 10am–1pm, 2pm–6pm, otherwise 10am–1pm, 3pm–7pm | 6 euros | temporary exhibitions in summer).*

FOOD & DRINK

LE 360° ☯
Take in the most spectacular views of Cannes, the sea and the Lérins Islands from the terrace of this exclusive restaurant at *Radisson Blu 1835 (134 rooms | 1, Blvd. Jean Hibert | tel. 04 92 99 73 00 | www.radissonblu.com | Expensive)* by the harbour. The prices for the Mediterranean

haute cuisine are relatively (!) moderate. *Tel. 04 92 99 73 20 | Expensive*

INSIDER TIP ▶ LE BISTROT GOURMAND
Conveniently located next to the Forville market its chef Guillaume Arragon offers

resented in *Rue d'Antibes*. Tantalizing the taste buds are delicatessens or *traiteurs* such as cheese specialist *Céneri & Fils* in *Rue Meynadier* in the pedestrian zone and the **INSIDER TIP ▶** Marché Forville market hall *(Tue–Sun)*. The flower mar-

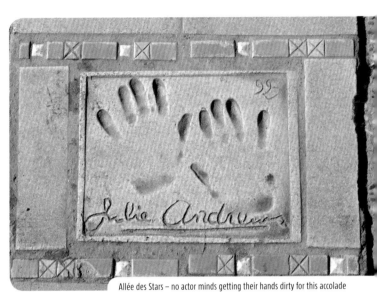

Allée des Stars – no actor minds getting their hands dirty for this accolade

excellent regional cuisine. *Closed for dinner Sun, Mon | 10, Rue du Docteur P. Gazagnaire | tel. 04 93 68 72 02 | www.bistrotgourmandcannes.fr | Budget–Moderate*

AUX BONS ENFANTS
This small restaurant between La Croisette and old town Cannes dates back to 1935 and is still serving loyal regulars its unpretentious regional dishes in traditional crockery. Cash only. *Closed Sun, Mon, Dec | 80, Rue Meynadier | Budget*

SHOPPING

The stores meet exclusive demands. Every conceivable fashion brand is rep-

ket is on the *Allées de la Liberté* by the harbour every morning and it makes way for a browsers' paradise on a Saturday and Sunday when it turns into a flea and antique market.

SPORTS & BEACHES

Cannes' most beautiful beaches lie on La Croisette and sections of beaches are accessible to the general public – not all are exclusive to the big hotels. Try *Les Thermes Marins (47, rue Georges Clémenceau | tel. 04 92 99 50 10 | www.lesthermesmarins-cannes.com)*, a modern thalassotherapy centre covering a 29,000 ft² area of the *Radisson Blu 1835*

Who said it's all bling bling in Cannes? Nonsense – you wouldn't believe how down-to-earth it is on the beach in the evening

hotel at the old harbour with direct access to the sea. All kinds of water sports from peddle boats to surfing to paragliding are available from *Majestic Ski Club (Blvd. de la Croisette | opposite Hotel Majestic | tel. 04 92 98 77 47)*.

ENTERTAINMENT

How to have a cheap time out in Cannes: get into your glad rags, grab a bottle of wine, and listen to the bands on the Croisette. And if you'd like to spend a little more, go to the numerous beach bars – or to the established clubs, from *Le Bâoli (daily in high season | Port Pierre Canto | Blvd. de la Croisette)* to *Vogue (Tue–Sun from 10pm | 20, Rue du Suquet)*.

WHERE TO STAY

3,14

Designer hotel with each floor dedicated to a different continent. Pool on the roof terrace, wellness area and an  organic restaurant. *96 rooms and suites | 5, Rue François Einesy | tel. 04 92 99 72 00 | www.314cannes.com | Expensive*

ALBERT I

Small hotel with oleanders on its shady patio. Only a ten minute walk from La Croisette. Free parking. *12 rooms | 68, Av. de Grasse | tel. 04 93 39 24 04 | www.hotel-albert1er-cannes.com | Moderate*

LE FLORIAN

Hotel in a quiet street only 100 m/328 ft from La Croisette with unassuming, but very clean rooms, some with balconies where breakfast is served. *20 rooms | closed Dec | 8, Rue du Commandant André | tel. 04 93 39 24 82 | www.hotel-leflorian.com | Moderate*

INFORMATION

Palais des Festivals | 1, Blvd. de la Croisette | tel. 04 92 99 84 22 | www.cannes-destination.fr

WHERE TO GO

LE CANNET (140–141 C–D4) (*ω N8*)

In 1926, artist Pierre Bonnard (born near Paris in 1867) decided to make his home in this little town (pop. 42,000) on the seven hills, and until his death in 1947 he lived at the *Villa Le Bosquet*. His years here were his most creative. The municipality, which adjoins Cannes to the north, purchased a former hotel and police department of 1908 and converted them into the **INSIDERTIP** *Musée Bonnard (Tue–Sun 10am–8pm | 7 euros | 16, Blvd. Sadi Carnot | www.museebonnard.fr)*. The first paintings by Pierre Bonnard were purchased for the museum in 2003. The museum stages changing exhibitions by representatives of Post-Impressionism. A ✍ *discovery trail* (approx. 2 hours) along the *Canal de la Siagne* that follows in the painter's footprints opens up views of Cannes, of the Lérins Islands and the Esterel mountains. Information: *Maison du Tourisme | Place Benidorm | www.lecannet-tourisme.fr*

ILES DE LÉRINS ★ (141 D5) (*ω N8*)

Are the monks real? Take the 20-minutes boat ride from the Promenade in Cannes over to ● *Saint-Honorat*, and you'll feel you as if you are in a different world. Vineyards, silent monks, and no cars. The Cistercian monks on the island – which is open to visitors during the day (only one restaurant, take your own food and water) – are famous for their wines and herb liqueur *(lerina)*. It is a lovely two-hour walk to the fortified tower on the southern point. Ferries daily from the Quai Max Laubeuf in Cannes. *Société Planaria (15 euros | tel. 04 92 98 71 38 | www.abbayedelerins.com)*.
Sainte-Marguerite is bigger than *Saint-Honorat* and has a *Circuit Botanique et Naturaliste* or educational garden and

the *Musée de la Mer* (April–Sept Tue–Sun 10.30am–1.15pm, 2.15pm–5.45pm, in winter Tue–Sun 10.30am–1.15pm, 2.15pm–4.45pm / 6 euros) which has archaeological and nautical displays. The *Fort Royal* is famous as the 17th century prison which held *The Man with the Iron Mask*. There are a few (relatively expensive) restaurants on the island, no accommodation. Trips across daily (15 minutes) from Cannes harbour. *Trans Côte d'Azur (13 euros | tel. 04 92 98 71 30 | www.trans-cote-azur.com)*

MANDELIEU-LA-NAPOULE (140 C4–5) (*ω M–N8*)

Town or countryside? If you can't decide, go to Mandelieu-la-Napoule (pop. 21,000), just ten minutes by train from Cannes. Its deep-red cliffs are perfect for hiking, the deep-blue sea for bathing. Worth a visit is the *Château de la Napoule*, a building that was restored by

LOW BUDGET

Le Chanteclair hotel (closed in Dec | 12, Rue Forville | tel. 04 93 39 68 88 | www.hotelchanteclair.com | Budget) directly next to the Forville market in Cannes is unpretentious with small but pristine rooms, 15 in all. Breakfast is served in a tranquil courtyard.

Since the ● *Museum of Photography* (Tue–Fri 10am–1pm, 2pm–6pm, Sat/Sun 11am–6pm | Porte Sarrazin) at the old town entrance of Mougins has stopped charging admission, visitor figures have skyrocketed. Look out for the photos that David Douglas Duncan took of Pablo Picasso.

American sculptor Henry Clews (1876–1937). In the summer months the *Henry Clews Muséum (Feb–beg. of Nov daily 10am–6pm, in winter Sat/Sun 10am–5pm, Mon–Fri 2pm–5pm | 6 euros with guided tour | www.chateau-lanapoule.com)* hosts exhibitions by American artists with sponsorships from the La Napoule Art Foundation. Information: *Av. Henry Clews | tel. 04 93 49 95 31 | www.ot-mandelieu.fr*

MOUGINS (140 C4) (*Ø N7*)

Picture-perfect best describes old town Mougins with its neat little houses and inviting squares. Mougins (pop. 20,000) 4 km/2.5 mi north was once larger than Cannes. Today the fortified town is a gourmet's delight. Top chefs David Chauvac of *le Mas Candille (46 rooms | restaurant closed Sun–Tue in winter | Blvd. Clément Rebouffel | tel. 04 92 28 43 43 | www.lemascandille.com | Expensive)* and Denis Fétisson of *L'Amandier (48, Av. Jean-Charles Mallet | tel. 04 93 90 91 | www.amandier.fr | Moderate–Expensive)* head the culinary list with both also offering cookery classes. Many of the town's restaurants follow in the footsteps of Roger Vergé considered the founder of *cuisine du soleil* Mediterranean cuisine. Beautiful rooms are available at *Mas de Mougins (4 rooms | 91, Av. Général de Gaulle | tel. 04 93 75 77 46 | www.lemasdemougins.com | Expensive)* where you will have your sumptuous breakfast served by the pool.

Mougins is also home to a private collection of Roman statues, antique weapons, works by Peter Paul Rubens and contemporary artists like Damien Hirst in the *Musée d'Art Classique (daily 10am–6pm / until 8pm in high summer | 32, rue du Commandeur | www.mouginsmusee.com | 12 euros)*. Admission to the ● *Museum to artist Maurice Gottlob (daily 10am–12.30pm, 2pm–6pm, until 7pm in high summer | 1, Place du Commandant Lamy)*, who met Auguste Rodin in Paris, is free. He settled in the South of France as a homeland artist and poet. Information: *18, Blvd. Courteline | tel. 04 93 75 87 67 | www.mougins.fr*

VALLAURIS-GOLFE-JUAN ★
(141 D4) (*Ø N8*)

Vallauris in the rolling hinterland hills 4 km/2.5 mi east of Cannes is an example of the extent to which art can become an economic force. It was here in 1946 that Pablo Picasso brought about a revival of the traditional ceramic art that had almost disappeared, and in 1952 he created his masterpiece *La Guerre et la Paix* (*War and Peace*) on display here: *Musée National (Wed–Mon 10am–noon, 2pm–5pm, in midsummer until 6pm | 4 euros | www.musee-picasso-vallauris.fr)*. His works can also be admired in the ceramics museum *(Musée Magnelli et Musée de la Céramique, Wed–Mon, 10am–noon and 2pm–5pm, until 6pm in midsummer | 4 euros)* that shows also works by the painter Alberto Magnelli *(1888–1971)*. Information: *Square du 8 mai 1945 | tel. 04 93 63 82 58 | www.vallauris-golfe-juan.com*

GRASSE

(140 C3) (*Ø M7*) **Nose to the front and go: if you don't become a fan of fragrances in ★ Grasse (pop. 51,000), it's your own fault. Outside the gates to the city, which isn't in the least bit posh, grow fields of roses, lilies and lily-of-the-valley.** The leather industry once flourished in the city – the leather gloves produced had an unpleasant odour and perfumes were the perfect solution. Grasse is ideally suited to the industry because

flowers and herbs thrive in its temperate microclimate. So it made sense to make the perfumes themselves. The Italian influence is evident in the architecture that graces the old town's narrow alleyways. The city has a long association with the Genoese Republic.

SIGHTSEEING

OLD TOWN

With its yellow, ochre, pink and blue houses, old town Grasse is lovely to stroll through. Go from the underground car park on the Place du Cours and take Rue Jean Ossola to get to *Notre-Dame-du-Puy*. The cathedral is an eclectic mix of medieval and rococo architecture and houses works by Peter Paul Rubens, a triptych by Louis Bréa and Jean-Honoré Fragonard's only religious painting. Head past the town hall (once the bishop's palace), to the beautiful *Place aux Herbes* with its colourful houses and then across to the *Place aux Aires* which was once the domain of the tanners. Today it is Grasse's market square where flowers and fresh produce are sold daily. Worth seeing is the magnificent 18th century façade of the *Hôtel Isnard*.

MUSÉE D'ART ET D'HISTOIRE DE PROVENCE

This superbly stocked museum of ethnography is housed in the palace of the 18th century Marquise de Clapiers-Cabris. *Daily 10am–7pm in summer, otherwise Wed–Mon 10.30am–5.30pm | free entrance | 2, Rue Mirabeau | www.musees degrasse.com*

MUSÉE INTERNATIONAL DE LA PARFUMERIE

The many different fragrances in this vast museum could well leave you feeling dizzy: after a guided tour, that fre-

quently crosses the town walls, visitors have dozens of fragrances in their noses. Grasse doesn't intend to leave you in any doubt that it is the international capital of perfume, and built its museum on an area of 37,000 ft^2 and in five buildings with 5000 exhibits. *Daily 10am–7pm in summer, otherwise*

Best-seller: Picasso helped Vallauris's ceramic art get off to a good start

Wed to Mon 10.30am–5.30pm | 4 euros | 2, Blvd. du Jeu de Ballon | www.musees degrasse.com

PERFUME FACTORIES ●

The big three perfume manufacturers, *Fragonard (20, Blvd. Fragonard | tel. 04 93 36 44 65 | www.fragonard. com), Galimard (73, Route de Cannes |*

tel. 04 93 09 20 00 | www.galimard.com)
and *Molinard (60, Blvd. Victor Hugo | tel. 0 49 33 01 62 | www.molinard.com)* offer free tours in English *(summer 9am– 6.30pm, winter 9am–12.30pm and 2pm– 6pm)*. It can take a professional up to two years to create a new fragrance. You can create your own in as little as two hours after the INSIDERTIP workshop Galimard offers visitors under professional guidance (also in English) *Studio des Fragrances (5, Route de Pégomas | tel. 04 93 09 20 00)*. You will be able to take your creation home with you right away (from 45 euros) and it will be kept on file in case you wish to re-order.

FOOD & DRINK

LA BASTIDE SAINT-ANTOINE ⤫
Top chef Jacques Chibois has been running this excellent gourmet restaurant in the south of Grasse. It also has sea views. *Open daily | 48, Av. Henri Dunant | tel. 04 93 70 94 94 | www.jacques-chibois. com | Expensive | also 16 rooms and suites | Expensive*

INSIDERTIP **LE CAFÉ DES MUSÉES**
At lunchtime, this little café with the mini terrace is right next door to the Musée International de la Parfumerie, a sure bet that serves Provencal specialities, fresh salads and vegetable tarts. *Closed Sun and evenings | 1, Rue Jean Ossole | tel. 04 92 60 99 00 | Budget*

SHOPPING

Shopping for perfume is an absolute must! Aside from the big name fragrance producers *Fragonard, Galimard* and *Molinard* there are *Guy Bouchara (14, Rue Marcel Journet)* and *Fleuron de Grasse (190, Route de Pégomas)* – both come highly recommended.

WHERE TO STAY

INSIDERTIP **AUBERGE DU VIEUX CHÂTEAU** ⤫
This hotel is located next to the church on the square in the medieval village of Cabris (pop. 500) around 5 km/3.1 mi west of Grasse and has a fabulous view of the sea and city. *4 rooms | Place du Panorama | tel. 04 93 60 50 12 | auberge duvieuxchateau.com | Moderate | with excellent restaurant | closed Mon, Tue | Expensive*

MANDARINA
Once a convent this hotel has stunning views of the the bay of La Napoule and the Lérins Islands from the ⤫ breakfast patio and some of the rooms. *35 rooms |*

Lavender? Mimosa? Or perhaps jasmine? No easy decision in Grasse

39, Av. Yves-Emmanuel Baudoin | tel. 04 93 36 10 29 | Moderate

L'OUSTAU DE L'AGACHON

Tranquil ✹ rooms set in a 17th century guest house in Cabris some with a view of the Esterel mountains. *5 rooms | closed Oct-March | 14, Rue de l'Agachon | Cabris, 8 km/5 mi east of Grasse on the D 11 | tel. 04 93 60 52 36 | www.cabris-chambres-hotes.com | Budget*

Parking at the Park + Ride at the station is free if you take the bus shuttle *Funix* (1.50 euros) to the city centre and show your ticket. *22, Cours Honoré Cresp | tel. 04 93 36 66 66 | www.grasse.fr*

WHERE TO GO

GOURDON ✹
(140 C2–3) (*ⁿ N6*)

The location of this Saracen village – (pop. 400) perched on a rock overhang 758 m/2487 ft above the river Loup and some 15 km/9.3 mi north-east of Grasse – is absolutely magnificent with breathtaking views over the valley. The castle built in the 13th and 17th century is privately owned and not open to the public. The village itself is an arts and crafts haven and home to perfume factory Galimard's *Boutique La Source Parfumée (Rue principale | tel. 04 93 09 68 23 | www.galimard.com)*. Information: *1, Place Victoria | tel. 08 11 81 10 67 | www.gourdon06.fr*

THE WEST COAST

Ochre at sunrise, bright red at noon, and crimson in the evening: the Esterel mountains to the west of Cannes are so lovely and so red. Walk around there, and you'll need a jerry can of water in the middle of summer: the rocks reflect the sunlight, making an ordinary walk like a hike through the desert. But on the bright side, all paths lead to a bay where you can bathe and cool down.

No one is allowed to build into the red cliffs anymore, but by the time the Coastal Protection Law was passed many B&B and hotels had been built. The streets are full at high season, but there's always plenty of space on the coastal path.

The French Riviera's west coast owes the economic success it is experiencing to mass tourism with all its pros and cons. There is an excellent hotel and restaurant infrastructure, but the downside is traffic jams in summer and an over-developed urban sprawl, not only along the coast but further inland.

FRÉJUS/ SAINT-RAPHAËL

(140 A–B6) (*ØØ L–M9*) Are the two Roman towns Saint-Raphaël and Fréjus two or one, one or two? Whatever, both have equally lovely beach casinos, sandy beaches and idyllic petanque

Azure sea, red rock and green mountains: the hustle and bustle of the coastal resorts, the restful calm of the foothills

pitches under shady plane trees. And with a combined population of just under 86,000, are almost the same size as Cannes.

Saint-Raphaël always used to be in the shadow of Fréjus (pop. 52,000), an important port in Roman times, and in the Middle Ages was a flourishing bishop's seat. Today it's almost a shame to see how much these two historic centres have succumbed to the same standard pleasures, including the obligatory bikini shops and ice cream cafés. However, the red hills and fine beaches in the surrounding area do help to compensate for this.

SIGHTSEEING

ARÈNES DE FRÉJUS

Everywhere you go in this city there is evidence of Roman ruins. The amphitheatre has been especially well preserved and with 10,000 seats is a popular venue for bullfights *(corrida)* and pop concerts. *Tue until Sun 9.30am–12.30pm, 2pm–6pm,*

Provides shade and creates a barrier to the beach bustle: the Gothic cloister of Fréjus

in winter Tue, Wed, Fri, Sat 9.30am–noon, 2pm–4.30pm | 2 euros

GROUPE EPISCOPAL ★

Fréjus has a perfect example of early gothic Provençal medieval architecture. The foundation of the baptistery *(baptistière)*, dating back to the 5th century, is one of the oldest religious monuments in France. The 12th century cathedral houses an altarpiece of Sainte-Marguerite by Jacques Durandi. Impressive too is the twin-storey cloister *(cloître)* with its fountain and garden. Fréjus' *La Tour Riculphe* Episcopal palace today houses the municipal offices. *Mid May–mid Aug daily 9am–6.30pm, otherwise Tue–Sun 9am–noon, 2pm–5pm | 5.50 euros | 58, Rue de Fleury*

FOOD & DRINK

BRASSERIE TRADITION ET GOURMANDISE

Right at the heart is a restaurant that serves Provençal cuisine on a pretty terrace and at good prices, especially at lunchtime. *Closed Sun | 6, Av. de Valescure | Saint-Raphaël | tel. 04 94 95 25 00 | www.labrasserietg.fr | Budget–Moderate*

LE MÉROU ARDENT

The "Fiery Sea Bass" a pleasant restaurant with a large terrace on the beach at Fréjus, serves mainly fish to classic recipes. *High summer closed Sat, Mon and Thu midday, otherwise closed Wed, Thu | 157, Blvd. la Libération | tel. 04 94 17 30 58 | Moderate*

SHOPPING

The large *Marché Provençal* with its array of foods, clothing, antiquities and bric-a-brac is held in Fréjus on Sundays on the *Boulevard d'Alger* and *Boulevard de la Libération*. A small market is held in the city's historical centre on a Wednesday and a Saturday. St-Raphaël holds a *food market* from Tuesday to Sunday on the *Place de la République* and *Place*

Victor Hugo, while the *fish market* runs daily from 7.30am until lunchtime in the old harbour.

SPORTS & BEACHES

The beaches at Fréjus and St-Raphaël go on forever. At Fréjus' new harbour the international diving centre *CIP de Port-Fréjus (April–Dec | Aire de carénage | tel. 04 94 52 34 99 | cip-frejus.com)* organises excursions and 'diving baptisms' for recreational diving. Fréjus has a 200-acre park, the *Base Nature, (midsummer daily 8am–8pm, otherwise 2pm–6pm | free entrance | Blvd. de la Mer)* directly on the sea with a supervised beach, cycling tracks, hiking trails, skate park and children's playground in the summer. The holiday resort in Cap Esterel has launched *Esterel Forme (Agay | tel. 04 94 82 52 34 | www.esterel-forme. com)*, a spa also open to day visitors for treatments, massage therapies and Turkish baths.

ENTERTAINMENT

Staint-Raphaël has a casino, bars and live clubs like *Coco Club* in the Santa Lucia harbour, while Fréjus has popular dance clubs like *L'Odyssée (Blvd. de la Libération)*, open every night in midsummer.

WHERE TO STAY

The best hotels are on the outskirts such as the fashionable Saint-Raphaël *suburb of Valescure*.

L'ARÉNA

Located nearby the ruins of a Roman arena, this pleasant hotel with beautiful garden and pool has charmingly decorated rooms and its restaurant is rated one of Fréjus' best. *39 rooms | closed Nov | 139–145, Rue du Général de Gaulle | Fréjus | tel. 04 94 17 09 40 | www.hotel-frejus-arena.fr | Expensive*

AUBERGE DE JEUNESSE

Frejus has the only youth hostel for far and wide, and because it's in the middle of a pine forest, has double beds, there's a frequent bus right to the beach and it's only a short walk to the old town,

It was the Middle Ages in Hyères when the Templars built their tower – without palm trees and bathers

it's a good choice. For the young-at-heart – that would be you! *101 beds | from 21 euros/night | 627, Chemin du Counillier | tel. 04 94 53 18 75 | www. hifrance.org*

L'OASIS

An unpretentious hotel in a 1950s building in a cul-de-sac. Only 150 m from the beach, with parking. *27 rooms | 71, Impasse Jean-Baptiste Charcot | Fréjus | tel. 04 94 51 50 44 | www.hotel-oasis. net | Budget*

WHERE TO GO

CAP DU DRAMONT (140 B6) *(M9)*
This outcrop 4 km/2.5 mi east is the beginning of the scenic road *Corniche d'Or* from Saint-Raphaël to Cannes. A coastal hike is one of the popular things to do here. The trail begins at the water sports centre on Dramont beach with its monument to commemorate the landing of US troops in 1944. It goes all the way to the ☀ lighthouse and the Camp Long bay *(2 hours there and back)*.

MASSIF DE L'ESTEREL ★
(140 B–C 5–6) *(M8–9)*
Red rock, green pines, turquoise sea and blue skies – the Massif de l'Esterel (north-east of Fréjus) is quite stunning. Deep ravines cut through the mountainous terrain with its 618 m/2028 ft high *Mont Vinaigre* all the way to the sea where waves break against the volcanic

rock cliffs. ✂ The magnificent hiking trails to the 452 m/1483 ft *Pic du Cap Roux* or 496 m/1627 ft *Pic de l'Ours* are best in the spring and autumn, when the maquis scrub is in full bloom. Information: *Office de Tourisme Saint-Raphaël*

HYÈRES-LES-PALMIERS

(142 B5) (*H11–12*) **Hyères (pop. 56,000) is the French Riviera's oldest seaside resort and with palm trees on every street it has a tropical feel to it – the iconic palms have even been included in its name.**
The English, Irish and Americans discovered the resort town in the 19th century, although it was only in the 20th century that its miles of beach were developed. Today the *old town*, with its Renaissance gates and *Tour Saint-Blaise* (a Knights Templar tower dating from the 13th century) is separated from the coastal resort Hyères-Plage by the airport.

SIGHTSEEING

JARDIN OLBIUS-RIQUIER
Palms and cacti, greenhouses, an outdoor animal enclosure and a lake. *Daily In summer 7.30am–8pm, in winter until 5pm | free entrance | Av. A. Thomas*

INSIDER TIP ▶ VILLA NOAILLES
Villa Noailles, the avant-garde coastal mansion of the art lovers Marie-Laure and Charles de Noailles, has been an icon for modern architecture since the 1920s. Man Ray made his first film here. Alberto Giacometti, Luis Buñuel and Jean Cocteau were once visitors. It houses the fashion and photography festival in April, temporary exhibitions in summer *(midsummer Wed–Sun 10am–noon, 4pm–7pm, otherwise Wed–Sun 10am–noon, 2pm–5pm | Montée de Noailles | www.villanoailles-hyeres.com)*. A footpath takes you up a hill to the ✂ ruins of *Château d'Hyères* that offers great panoramic views.

FOOD & DRINK

LA COLOMBE
2.5 km/1.6 mi further to the west, Mediterranean cuisine is served on the lovely terrace of an inner courtyard in summer. *Closed for lunch Mon, Tue, Sat in July and Aug, otherwise closed Sat for lunch and Sun/Mon evening | 663, Route de Toulon | tel. 04 94 35 35 16 | www.restaurantla colombe.com | Moderate–Expensive*

THE RIVIERA IS MAKING AN EFFORT

Something the hoteliers and restaurant owners on the chic coast haven't yet seen: after the terrorist attack on Nice Promenade in July 2016, they had to tout for business for the first time. Previously, visitors had come unbidden, but now this stopped. And the French Riviera had to make an effort. Today, countless tourists agree: service all along the coast has improved since then, and the bargains are better. The advertising campaign „I love Nice" *(ilove.nice.fr)* encourages people to take part, and every day scores of private photos taken on the French Riviera are seen in the social media.

LE DÉSIRÉ

A small restaurant near the town hall that serves Mediterranean cuisine on beautifully decorated plates. Closed Wed, *Sat noon and Sun evening | 13, Rue Crivelli | tel. 04 94 20 27 38 | www.restaurant-ledesire.com | Budget–Moderate*

LES OMBRELLES

On the road from Hyères to Giens, just 50 m/164 ft from the beach, a German chef lovingly prepares Provençal meals at good prices. Beer garden. *Daily from 7pm | Quartier de la Capte | tel. 04 94 01 31 72 | Budget–Moderate | also has 4 basic rooms | Budget*

ENTERTAINMENT

Aside from the casino in old town Hyères there are a number of clubs like *Le Pink (closed Mon–Wed | 85, Av. de l'Arrogante, on La Capte beach)* or *One Again (Wed,* Fri–Sun from midnight | 494, Rue Nicéphore Niepce, at the airport)*

LOW BUDGET

The *bateau-bus-téléphérique* pass costs 6 euros and is available at the *Office de Tourisme* in Toulon. Included is the boat trip across the bay to the Saint-Mandrier peninsula, all bus routes in the city, as well as the cable car up Mont Faron.

Access to the beach is free for pedestrians on the Saint-Tropez peninsula and in Ramatuelle. Parking fees apply everywhere in summer. An exception is *Escalet* beach which is also demarcated on the *coastal hiking trail (sentier littoral)* – you may come across quiet isolated beaches on the trail also in high season.

WHERE TO STAY

BOR

Modern seaside hotel some 4 km/2.5 mi to the south of the city with its own beach – a short walking distance from Port Saint-Pierre. *20 rooms | closed Dec–March | 3, Allée Emile Gérard | tel. 04 94 58 02 73 | www.hotel-bor.com | Expensive*

DOMAINE LES FOUQUES ☘ ⊛

This organic wine and poultry estate has a superb view of the sea and of Porquerolles island. Three *gîtes* with patios and a swimming pool can be rented on a weekly basis *(accommodates 4 people | July/Aug 675 euros, June/Sept 485 euros, off-peak season 360 euros)*. The estate sells its own organic products. *20 rooms | 1405, Chemin des Borrels | tel. 04 94 65 68 19 | fouques-bio.com*

DU SOLEIL

This picturesque Provençal hotel overgrown with ivy is at the foot of the medieval castle in a small alleyway by Hyères' city wall. Serves an excellent breakfast. *20 rooms | Rue du Rempart | tel. 04 94 65 16 26 | www.hoteldusoleil.com | Moderate*

INFORMATION

Av. de Belgique | tel. 04 94 01 84 50 | www.hyeres-tourisme.com

WHERE TO GO

GIENS (142 B6) (𝄞 H12)

Two 4 km/2.5 mi stretches of sand or *tombolo* connect the former island of Giens with the mainland. The lagoon between them was a salt marsh until 1996, and today the area is a protected habitat. Coastal conservation authorities are doing their best to maintain its ecological balance especially for the bird life under threat from the sand erosion of the western stretch. The village of Giens is on the peninsula with its small harbour Port de Niel. From the ☀ fort ruins you will have an excellent view of the islands and mainland. Département Var has one of the INSIDER TIP most beautiful sections of coastal hiking trails. The 6.5 km/4 mi stretch from the small La Madrague har-

ture reserve with a botanical information centre, vineyards and accommodation: *Mas du Langoustier (50 rooms | closed Oct–mid April | 3.5 km/2.2 mi west of the harbour | tel. 04 94 58 30 09 | www. langoustier.com | Expensive)* has two restaurants. The island is only 7 km/4.4 mi and 3 km/1.9 mi wide and easy to explore on foot or by bicycle (bicycles can be hired in Porquerolles village). The hike from the harbour to the lighthouse in the south will take about an hour and a half.

Heavenly Porquerolles with its pretty harbour becomes a victim of its own beauty in summer

bour in the west of the peninsula to the Plage de l'Arbousière will take a seasoned hiker a good two hours.

ILES D'OR ★
(142–143 B–E6) (*⌕ H–K12*)

If you've ever seen the film "Welcome to the Sticks", you'll know that all the French dream of working on the heavenly island of *Porquerolles*. Like *Port-Cros* and *Levant,* it is one of the Iles d'Hyère or Iles d'Or that form part of the Massif des Maures, the cliffs of which all have a golden shimmer. *Porquerolles* is a na-

In 1963 *Port-Cros* became one of France's first national parks. Turning it into a reserve has allowed the 4 km/2.5 mi by 2.5 km/1.6 mi ft island with its 600 m/ 1969 ft wide stretch of water separating it from the mainland to maintain its splendour. Hiking trails take you into the *Vallon de la Solitude*, there is a plant trail or *Sentier Botanique* and it is at the *Plage de la Palud* where you will find the *Sentier Sous-Marin*, the first underwater trail for snorkellers.

The ferry to Porquerolles takes 20 minutes. Tickets at *La Tour Fondue (Gare*

Maritime | tel. 04 94 58 21 81 | www.tlv-tvm.com | 19.50 euros) in the Giens peninsula. Ferries to Port-Cros leave from Hyères harbour *(Port d'Hyères | tel. 04 94 57 44 07 | www.tlv-tvm.com | 28.10 euros).* Information: *Bureau d'Information de Porquerolles (tel. 04 94 58 33 76 | www.porquerolles.com); Bureau d'Informations du Parc (tel. 04 94 01 40 72 | www.portcrosparcnational.fr/accueil)*

MASSIF DES MAURES

(142–143 B–E 2–5) *(ᗡ H–K 9–11)* **If you like playing Cops and Robbers, head to the Maures Massif: its dense forests of oak, chestnut and cork oak trees is perfect for playing hide-and-seek.**

Thieves and small-time crooks used to hide out here, but today visitors can safely stroll to the highest cliffs and visit the Franciscan monastery of ⚜ *Notre-Dame-des-Anges*. The view from here across the mountains and sea is absolutely spectacular. The name of the mountain in Provençal means 'sombre forest'.

TOWNS IN THE MASSIF DES MAURES

BORMES-LES-MIMOSAS
(143 D5) *(ᗡ J11)*
The town (pop. 7100) owes the descriptive double-barrelled name it adopted (in 1968) to the mimosa trees that blossom here all in yellow in February. With its steep alleyways, abundance of flowers, eucalyptus, oleander and cypress trees and perched high up on the Massif des Maures, Bormes-les-Mimosas is a feast for the eyes. There are about 17 km/10.6 mi of beaches around *Fort Brégançon* 10 km/6.2 mi away (the offi-

cial residence of the French State President since 1968) as well as the *Plage de l'Estagnol (Easter–Oct | parking fee 8 euros*) with its white sands and pine forests. The gourmet restaurant in the village is run by Gil Renard at *La Tonnelle (Jul/Aug midday, otherwise closed Wed and mid-Nov to mid-Dec | Place Gambetta | tel. 04 94 71 34 84 | www.la-tonnelle-bormes.com | Moderate)* or *Lou Portaou (in summer only open for dinner, closed all day Mon and on Tue evening | 1, Cubert des Poètes | tel. 04 94 64 86 37 | Moderate)* with its medieval vaulted stone terrace. In ⚜ the old part of town is the newly renovated *Hôtel Bellevue (17 rooms | 14, Place Gambetta | tel. 04 94 71 15 15 | www.bellevuebormes.com | Budget)* with its expansive view of the sea *(with restaurant | Budget*). Information: *1, Place Gambetta | tel. 04 94 01 38 38 | www.bormeslesmimosas.com*

INSIDER TIP COLLOBRIÈRES
(142 C4) *(ᗡ J10)*
Pick up your basket and head to the chestnut harvest: these delicious brown tree fruits taste better in Collobrières (pop. 1700) than anywhere else. Because people used to live off the cork oak and chestnuts, traditionally they are turned into confectionery, jams and cakes. For instance, at the *Confiserie Azuréenne (Blvd. Koenig | www.confiserieazureenne.com).* The simple family *Hôtel-Restaurant des Maures (10 rooms | 19, Blvd. Lazare-Carnot | tel. 04 94 48 07 10 | www.hoteldesmaures.fr | Budget)* serves excellent Provençal home cooking. Regional fare is also served at **INSIDER TIP** *La Petite-Fontaine (closed on Sun evening, Mon | 1, Place de la République | tel. 04 94 48 00 12 | Budget–Moderate).* Advance dinner reservations. Information: *Blvd. Charles Caminat | tel. 04 94 48 04 10 | www.collobrieres-tourisme.com*

LA GARDE-FREINET (143 E3) (*Ⓜ K10*)

Once a Saracen retreat, today it is a pretty resort town amid cork oak and chestnut forests. This is an ideal base from which to explore the Massif des Maures. Take a walk (45 minutes) to the ⚹ ruins of *Fort Freinet* for a stunning view of the town. La Garde-Freinet (pop. 1800) is the gateway to the northern Massif des Maures. 14 km/8.7 mi to the west, through cork oak forests and en route to Le Gonfaron (see p. 116) lies the wine estate **INSIDER TIP** *Domaine de la Fouquette (4 rooms | open April–Oct | 1, Route de Gonfaron | tel. 04 94 73 08 45 | domaine-delafouquette.com | Budget)* set in idyllic surrounds. Dinner only after reservation in advance – meals served from almost exclusively home grown produce and the estate's own wine (*Moderate*). Information: *Point Infos Tourisme de la Garde-Freinet (chapelle Saint Jean) | tel. 04 94 56 04 93 | www.lagardefreinet-tourisme.com*

GRIMAUD ⚹ (143 E3) (*Ⓜ K10*)

Nestled beneath the ruins of an 11th century House of Grimaldi castle is one of the most beautiful towns in the Massif des Maures. Grimaud has lovely shaded squares, narrow alleyways and magnificent views. Over 50 years, the Girard family has cooked itself a good reputation with the region's connoisseurs at *Les Santons (closed Sun evening, Mon, Wed | 743, Route Nationale | tel. 04 94 43 21 02 | www.restaurant-les-santons.fr | Expensive)*. Auskunft: *15, Route départementale 558 | tel. 04 94 55 43 83 | www.grimaud-provence.com*

LE LAVANDOU (143 D5) (*Ⓜ J11*)

Once the sleepy fishing harbour to Bormes-les-Mimosas, where virtually no foreigners ventured, this town's (pop. 5800) tourism ascent has been quite phenomenal. Its influx of 100,000 visi-

When autumn starts to peep around the corner, it's time to celebrate the chestnut

tors every year has had a significant impact on the development of the region. There are dozens of hotels and plenty of campsites, not surprising given its many sought after beaches: *Aiguebelle, Cap Nègre, Pramousquier, Layet* and *Rossignol*. In winter Le Lavandou reverts back to a ghost town. Information: *Quai Gabriel Péri | tel. 04 94 00 40 50 | www.lelavandou.eu*

SPORTS & BEACHES

There is no shortage of hiking trails in the Massif des Maures – a good example is the GR 90 from Collobrières to the Carthusian monastery **INSIDER TIP** *Monastère de la Verne (Wed–Mon 11am–*

6pm, in winter 11am–5pm | closed Jan | 6 euros. Most of its buildings date from the 17th and 18th century. Special routes are demarcated for cyclists.

WHERE TO GO

CORNICHE DES MAURES ★ ☼
(143 D–E 4–5) (*Ø J–K11*)
Take the D 559 along the spectacular coast and head east towards *Cavalière* to the sandy beach between Pointe du Layet and Cap Nègre which is shielded from the mistral. After some 6 km/3.7 mi there is the INSIDER TIP *Domaine du Rayol (in summer Tue–Sun 9.30am–12.30pm and 2.30pm–6.30pm, in winter Tue–Sun 9.30am–12.30pm and 2pm–5.30pm |* 10.50 euros | *www.domainedurayol.org*), a botanical trail established by a Parisian banker in 1910 that takes you through trees, bushes and cacti from around the world. In summer there is the *Sentier Sous-Marin*, an underwater trail in the bay of Le Rayol. Continue on the road via Cavalaire-sur-Mer and you will reach *La Croix-Valmer* with one of the Mediterranean's delightful beaches – *Gigaro*.

SAINT-TROPEZ

(143 F3) (*Ø L10*) **What a surprise:** ★ **Saint-Tropez is a tiny town! Because countless jet-setters and yacht owners have made the harbour town famous all over the world, most people imagine Saint-Tropez to be a huge centre. But far from it – only about 5000 people live there. And yet it still became famous simply because so many beautiful and rich people couldn't possibly be wrong: Saint-Tropez lies in a protected bay, wine is grown on the surround-ing hills, and the sandy beaches are the very finest.**

The real fame of the small village of Saint-Tropez, which has been an autonomous republic from the 15th–17th century, started with the release of Roger Vadim's 1956 film *And God Created Woman* starring Brigitte Bardot, which was filmed in the bay of La Ponche. The film turned Saint-Tropez into an international destination, particularly for the new jet set crowd. Today, Paris Hilton, Madonna and Bono meet mainly in summer, and only in the exclusive clubs. Some 80,000 come to the town every day, and fine vast motor yachts in the harbour, hefty prices, and noise and bustle in the discos. However, once the holiday is over, Saint-Tropez is restored to its customary beauty. The holidays over, it reverts to its pristine beauty and you will see the locals resurface for a relaxed game of *pétanque* – a type of boules – on the *Place des Lices*.

SIGHTSEEING

OLD TOWN

Take a walk through old town Saint-Tropez, along past the church with its conspicuous ochre-coloured tower, to the *Place aux Herbes* market square and afterwards up to the ☀ citadel from where you will get an excellent view of the town and Gulf of Saint-Tropez.

HARBOUR

The sea is the heart of Saint-Tropez – even though it is not always visible in summer because of so many yachts. The harbour is also home to one of the world's most famous cafés, the *Sénéquier (*with its distinctive red décor) which remains a popular meeting place for the international crowd all year round.

MUSÉE DE L'ANNONCIADE ★

One of France's most spectacular art museums is housed in a former chapel right by the harbour of Saint-Tropez. On show: works by Paul Signac, Georges Seurat, Henri Matisse, Kees van Dongen, Albert Marquet and Henri Manguin. *Wed–Mon 10am–1pm, 2pm–6pm | 5 euros | 2, Rue de l'Annonciade*

FOOD & DRINK

LE GIRELIER

This 'fisherman's hut' on the harbour has experienced a revival. Serves seafood specialities. *Closed Nov–mid March | Quai Jean Jaurès | tel. 04 94 97 03 87 | www. legirelier.fr | Moderate–Expensive*

LA TABLE DU MARCHÉ

Christophe Leroy, a dynamic figure among the jet set of Saint-Tropez, has moved his bistro to the alleyways between

View of St-Tropez harbour at twilight

the harbour and church. Light snacks, full meals and Asian specialities. *11, Rue des Commerçants | tel. 04 94 97 01 25 | www.christophe-leroy.com |* Budget–Moderate

VILLA BELROSE ☆☆

This top restaurant with chef de cuisine Thierry Thiercelin lies on a hill near Gassin with breathtaking views of the Gulf of Saint-Tropez. *Closed end Oct–Mar | Blvd. des Crètes Gassin | tel. 04 94 55 97 97 | www.villa-belrose.com |* Expensive *| also has 40 rooms |* Expensive

SHOPPING

All the global luxury brands are available here. Rue Clémenceau has been famous for its *sandales tropéziennes* since 1927 – a pair will set you back around 85 euros. For the sweet tooth, the speciality you absolutely have to try while in Saint-Tropez is the calorie-rich cream *tarte tropézienne* sold in the store by the same name *(Place des Lices)*.

SPORTS & BEACHES

The town of *Ramatuelle* is where you need to head to for legendary beaches like Pampelonne and their famous bars.

ENTERTAINMENT

Nowhere else in France you will find as many discos and clubs per number of residents. The jet set, stars and models hang out at *Les Caves du Roy (Av. Maréchal Foch)* in Le Byblos hotel.

WHERE TO STAY

LOU CAGNARD

This small Provençal hotel with a 100 year old fig tree is within walking distance

of the harbour and the Place des Lices. Minimum stay in summer is one week. *19 rooms | closed Nov–Feb | 18, Av. Paul Roussel | tel. 04 94 97 04 24 | www.hotel-lou-cagnard.com |* Moderate

LA PONCHE ☆☆

This luxury hotel has plenty of charm and is located in the fishing quarter with a view of the bay. Excellent value for money restaurant *(Moderate)*. *18 rooms | closed Nov–mid Feb | Port des Pêcheurs | tel. 04 94 97 02 53 | www.laponche.com |* Expensive

INFORMATION

Quai Jean Jaurès | tel. 08 92 68 48 28 | www.sainttropeztourisme.com or Maison du Tourisme (Carrefour de la Foux | Gassin | tel. 04 94 55 22 00 | www.golfe-saint-tropez-information.com)

WHERE TO GO

PORT-GRIMAUD ★ ☻
(143 E3) (*∅ K10*)

This artificial resort marina with canals, bridges and colourful houses 6 km/ 3.7 mi from Saint-Tropez was created in 1966 by architect François Spoerry. He developed the marshland in the bay of Saint-Tropez with a concept for environmentally-friendly tourism. The resort is a rare example of how new buildings can blend into the environment unobtrusively and it has aged gracefully. It is not often that you find waterways for roads and residents that can sail right up to their front door in a boat. Visitors must leave their cars in a car park north of the village.

RAMATUELLE ★ (143 F4) (*∅ L11*)

This is a typical Provençal fortress town. Located 7 km/4.4 mi from Saint-Tropez in the middle of the peninsula it is home to 2300 residents whose quaint houses wind their way up against the hill. A *Festival de Théâtre* is held here every summer in honour of prominent French actor Gérard Philipe (1922–59).

Ramatuelle is synonymous with the legendary beaches and beach clubs that the Saint-Tropez peninsula is famous for: *Plage de Pampelonne* – with its *Club 55 (43, Blvd. Patch)* founded in the 1950s and the ancestor of all the beach clubs; *Key West Beach (Blvd. Patch)* and *Nikki Beach (Route de l'Epi)*. Not so good: club owners are fighting against the conservation zone being extended and the beaches being made smaller. In the long-term, though, there will be fewer mattresses in the bay, and in return more birds will be able to start nesting.

A quiet alternative to the lively hotels that Saint-Tropez is known for, is *Leï Souco* guest house on a wine estate *(10 rooms | April–beginning Sept | Route des Plages | D 63 | tel. 04 94 79 80 22 | www.leisouco.com | Moderate–Expensive)*. Launched in 1969 it is regarded as a pioneer for *chambres d'hôtes*.

For an impressive view of the sea, peninsula and Massif des Maures head to the ⚡ viewing point above *Les Moulins de Paillas* between the towns of Ramatuelle and *Gassin*. Although stunning Gassin can be something of a tourist trap. Information: *Place de l'Ormeau | tel. 04 98 12 64 00 | www.ramatuelle-tourisme.com*

La Tarte Tropézienne with reed-slim customers. So who eats the *gateaux*?

SAINTE-MAXIME (143 F3) (*ω L10*)

This old fishing village (pop. 14,000) lies opposite Saint-Tropez on the other side of the bay. It has become a year-round swimming resort and is a good alternative to the permanently overcrowded and expensive jet set Saint-Tropez. If you want to avoid the unrelenting traffic jams on the coastal road there is ● **INSIDER TIP** a ferry service: *Transports Maritimes MMG (April–Oct | return trip 13.50 euros | www.bateaux verts.com)*. Information: *1, Promenade Aymeric Simon-Lorière | tel. 0 82 62 83 83 (*) | www.sainte-maxime.com*

TOULON

(142 A5) (🗺 F–G11) **The biggest, the most impressive and the ugliest ships in the Mediterranean lie in Toulon: France's biggest military harbour also takes vast cargo ships, but otherwise is pretty. Although you won't find the jetset here, it has affordable markets and restaurants that serve freshly caught squid.**

Count the ships. Or the cranes. Or just enjoy the views on the cable car to Mont Faron

The capital of the Département Var (pop. 170,000) was partly destroyed in World War II. However, the town has been revitalised and today it is not only the locals who enjoy its purpose built INSIDER TIP *beaches in Mourillon*, with their parks and playgrounds, bars and restaurants.

SIGHTSEEING

OLD TOWN AND HARBOUR

The promenade on the Quai Cronstadt with its restaurants and cafés has been restored to its former glory, and sections of the old town north of the harbour are pedestrian precincts with inviting squares like *Place Raimu* with its life-size bronze card players, *Place Victor Hugo* with its 19th century theatre, *Place Ledeau*, a leafy spot in the city centre and the *Cours Lafayette* with its Provençal market *(Tue–Sun morning)*.

MONT FARON

584 m/1916 ft above sea level lies the ★ Mont Faron limestone peak with spectacular views across the entire bay of Toulon. The cable car or INSIDER TIP *téléphérique* for the mountain leaves from Boulevard Amiral Vence *(Bus No. 40 | closed Mon and in very windy conditions | 7 euros)*. At the top is a memorial museum to the August 1944 Allied landing *(Tue–Sun 10am–noon and 2pm–5.30pm | 4 euros)* and a feline breeding zoo *(daily 10am–6.30pm, in winter until 5.30pm | 9 euros, combi-ticket zoo/téléphérique 14 euros)*.

CITY **WHERE TO START?**
Harbour: stroll along the seaside promenade with its bars and restaurants along the edge of the magnificent Mediterranean bay of Toulon. On the opposite side of the road lies old town Toulon with its narrow alleyways and pretty squares. The car park at the stadium and shopping mall **Mayol** (*Blvd. Dutasta, 1.90 m/6.2 ft max.*) is within easy walking distance from the harbour and old town. There is also the relatively small **Le Port** car park directly by the sea.

MUSÉE D'HISTOIRE NATURELLE

The stuffed tiger nicknamed *Clem* is the symbol for the natural history museum, which focuses on raising awareness of the region's fauna and mineral wealth. Clem was born at the zoo on Mont Faron and was the mascot for the aircraft carrier Clémenceau stationed in Toulon until it was decommissioned 1997. *Mon–Fri 9am–6pm, Sat/Sun 11am–6pm | free entrance | 113, Blvd. Maréchal Leclerc*

FOOD & DRINK

MARCHÉ DU COURS LAFAYETTE

You can get the best finger food on the market at the Cours Lafayette. The atmosphere is amazing. And delicious, for instance, is the *cade*, a waffle made from chickpea flour, or *chichi frégie*, a rather greasy but unbelievably light kind of shortbread biscuit. *Tue-Sun 7.30am–12.30pm*

AU SOURD

For over 150 years, this establishment has been an institution in the old town of Toulon and serving fish specialities.

It's lovely on the terrace in summer. *Closed Sun, Mon | 10, Rue Molière | tel. 04 94 92 28 52 | www.ausourd.com | Moderate*

WHERE TO STAY

BONAPARTE

On the western edge of the old town overlooking the Place d'Armes, this hotel is the former residence of Napoleon. No lift or air conditioning. *22 rooms | 16, Rue Anatole France | tel. 04 94 93 07 51 | www.hotel-bonaparte.com | Budget*

GRAND HÔTEL DAUPHINÉ

Renovated hotel with tastefully decorated rooms on the pedestrian precinct 50 m/164 ft from Peiresc car park. *55 rooms | 10, Rue Berthelot | tel. 04 94 92 20 28 | www.grandhoteldauphine. com | Budget*

INFORMATION

12, Place Louis Blanc | tel. 04 94 18 53 00 | www.toulontourisme.com

WHERE TO GO

LE PRADET (142 A5) (*M G11*)

This coastal resort town (pop. 11,000) 9 km/5.6 mi east has five excellent swimming beaches: *Pin de Galle, Monaco, Bonnettes, Garonne* and *Oursinières*. A coastal path links them all. Visit the impressive *Musée de la Mine de Cap-Garonne (open daily 2pm–5pm during the French school holidays, Jul/Aug 2pm–5.30pm, otherwise Wed, Sat, Sun 2pm–5pm | 6.50 euros | www.mine-capgaronne.fr)*, a mining museum housed in an old copper mine at the most southerly tip. Information: *Place du Général de Gaulle | tel. 04 94 21 71 69 | www.lepradet-tourisme.fr*

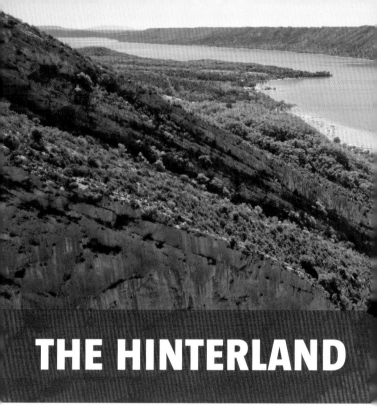

THE HINTERLAND

Machos on the French Riviera say that the farther you go into the hinterland, the more rustic the women are. As stupid as this saying is, in the *arrière-pays*, women trade their stilettos for hiking books, and well-fed farmers' wives replace the dangerously anorexic models seen on the coast. Goatherds, olive farmers and dropouts from societies from all over the world find their dreams come true here, in the unspoilt countryside.

It takes tourists 90 minutes to get from the beaches up the 2000-m/7000-ft mountains, where it's cool in summer and snowy in winter, but always almost overwhelmingly wild. The only thing the villages seem to share with the French Riviera is the language. Petanque and the local brasserie play the main role. And because there's

been virtually no new building for decades, they all seem to have retained their original character in the typical, basic stone dwellings. The deep, spectacular ravines carved by the Estéron, Loup and Verdon rivers make the area perfect for outdoor enthusiasts and are ideal for canoeing, kayaking and extreme mountaineering.

LES ALPES MARITIMES

(136–137 A–F 1–5) (*M–Q 2–6*)

From the palm-lined coastline it is only 50 km/30 mi or so to the coastal Alps (Alpes Maritimes) with peaks over 3000 m/9843 ft high.

Quiet villages, holy mountains and valleys
to marvel at: even wolves have been spotted
in the quiet hinterlands of the French Riviera

The mountain range of the Nice and Monaco hinterland with the Vésubie, Bévéra and Roya river valleys is the French Riviera's landscape of dramatic contrasts.

WHERE TO GO IN THE ALPES MARITIMES

PARC NATIONAL DU MERCANTOUR

(136–137 A–F 1–3) (ϖ M–Q 2–5)

With its peak at 2873 m/9426 ft *Mont Bégo* may not necessarily be the highest mountain, but it is definitely the nature reserve's most sacred, its name means 'divine' in Ligurian. Hares, foxes, eagles and ibexes still roam here and so do wolves (as of 1992), to the delight of nature conservationists but to the chagrin of the shepherds. Mercantour with its 265 mi² area stretching from Sospel in the south, the Italian border in the north and the Col d'Allos in the west, became France's most recent national park in 1979 and works closely with Italy's *Parco delle Alpi Marittime*.

The parish church of Saorge is full of the entire range of baroque glory

The park has more than 600 km/373 mi of signposted hiking trails. There are a dozen or so mountain huts (be sure to book in peak season!) in a landscape that still remains largely unspoilt. Information: *Les Iris | Rue K. Serrurier | Saint-Martin-Vésubie | tel. 04 93 03 23 15 | www.mercantour.eu*. Information and suggestions for tourists are also available from the *Maisons Du Parc*, e.g. in *Saint-Etienne-de-Tinée (Quartier de l'Ardon | tel. 04 93 02 42 27), Valberg (Le Ciastel | Maison Valberganne | tel. 04 93 02 58 23)* and *Tende (103, Av. du 16 Septembre 1947 | tel. 04 93 04 67 00)*.

SAORGE ★ (137 E3) (*Q4*)

Saorge is the hippy village of the French Riviera: ☻ organic biscuits, farmers with dreadlocks and the highest election results for candidates from the left. The **INSIDER TIP** local honeys are available to sample and purchase from the communal *Miellerie (daily from 2pm–6pm| Place Ciapane | tel. 04 93 04 55 38).*

Stroll through and visit the parish church *Église Saint-Claude* with its baroque interior. The façade of the Franciscan monastery, the *Monastère de Saorge* built in the 17th century, has recently been restored. Between the village and the monastery you will find **INSIDER TIP** *Lou Pountin (closed Tue, Wed | 56, Rue Lieutenant Jean Revelli | tel. 04 93 04 54 90 | www.loupountin.fr | Budget)*, a restaurant serving lots of ☻ organic products in a comfortably cool dining room or on its sunny terrace. Information: *Mairie (town hall) (Av. Docteur Joseph Davéo | tel. 04 93 04 51 23)*

VALLÉE DES MERVEILLES ★
(137 D–E2) (*P–Q4*)

The 40,000 or so rock carvings found in the Vallée des Merveilles at the foot of Mont Bégo in the Parc National du Mercantour remain as much of a mystery today as when they were first discovered in the 17th century. In the last century researchers began a systematic study of them. Carvings like *le sorcier*, supposedly the image of a sorcerer, is one of the better known and is quite rare in that it depicts a person. The bulk of the carvings date back to the Bronze Age between 2800 and 1300 BC. The only way to access the open-air carvings off the GR 52 hiking trail is with an experienced guide. Information at *Association des Guides, Accompagnateurs et Amis des Alpes Méridionales (Bureau de la Haute Vésubie | Saint-Martin-Vésubie | tel. 04 93 03 26 60* or *Parc National du Mercantour)*. Or you can visit the over 10,000 ft² exhibition space dedicated to the findings at the ● *Musée des Merveilles (midsummer daily 10am–6.30pm, May, June, Oct Wed–Mon 10am–6.30pm, winter Wed–Mon 10am–5pm | free entrance | Av. du 16 sept. 1947 | Tende | www. museedesmerveilles.com)*.

The hotel *Le Mirval (18 rooms | closed Nov–March | 3, Rue Vincent Ferrier | tel. 04 93 04 63 71 | www.lemirval.com | Budget)* in *La Brigue* also organises excursions into the valley. The pretty mountain village with its square and 13th century Saint-Martin church has retained its Italian heritage. Just 4 km/2.5 mi outside is the chapel INSIDER TIP▶ *Notre-Dame-des-Fontaines (May–Oct daily 10am–12.30pm, 2pm–5.30pm | 3 euros | www.labrique.fr)* with frescos by 15th century Piedmontese painters Giovanni Baleison and Giovanni Canavesio.

VALLÉE DE VÉSUBIE
(136 B–C4) (*m O5*)

The locals call their Vésubie valley „mini Switzerland", and in fact they have a point: green meadows, unspoilt villages and 3000-m/10,000-ft mountains do indeed resemble the alpine landscapes of Switzerland. Just after Saint-Jean-la-Rivière, the Vésubie river provides a beautiful natural spectacle as it passes through the ★ *Gorges de la Vésubie* flanked by steep multicoloured rock walls. From the D 2565 turn off into the D 32 to *La Madone d'Utelle,* a 9th century pilgrimage site founded by mariners. The views of the mountains and sea from the ⛰ *Plateau de la Madone d'Utelle,* a plattform at 1174 m/3852 ft, are unforgettable.

★ **Saorge**
A touch of Tibet in the Roya valley
→ **p. 84**

★ **Vallée des Merveilles**
Valley of wonder and mystery: rock carvings in the Parc National du Mercantour → **p. 84**

★ **Gorges de la Vésubie**
Nice's dramatic hinterland terrain – a spectacular river gorge → **p. 85**

★ **Gorges du Verdon**
One of Europe's deepest gorges
→ **p. 87**

★ **Moustiers-Sainte-Marie**
The village with a silver star → **p. 88**

★ **Musée de Préhistoire des Gorges du Verdon**
In the footsteps of humanity in Quinson's museum → **p. 89**

★ **Abbaye du Thoronet**
Provençal masterpiece of the Romanesque period → **p. 90**

★ **Train des Pignes**
No less than 33 bridges are traversed on the legendary steam train ride → **p. 93**

MARCO POLO HIGHLIGHTS

CASTELLANE

(134 B5) (*K5*) **A place for the hyper-active: Castellane offers hiking through the gorges, swimming in the lake, canyoning, Provençal cuisine and, of course, a *citadelle (Petra Castellana)*.**

Today, the small town (pop. 1600), which is located at the Route Napoléon that leads from the sea to the Alps, is the perfect base to set out from to explore the Verdon Gorge.

SIGHTSEEING

OLD TOWN
The small village with its narrow alleyways has managed to retain a few of its architectural gems even though there is not much left of the old castle. The city gate *Porte Royale* with its clock tower *Tour de l'Horloge* and the five-sided *Tour Pentagonale*, are all that remain of the old town wall.

BERGERIE DE FAUCON
Animals heal young people on this farm, and as a visitor you are guaranteed to feel the Zen effect of camels, deer and cattle. *Daily 2pm–5pm | free entrance | on the road between La Palud-sur-Verdon and Rougon*

NOTRE-DAME-DU-ROC 🔆
From the parish church hike along the old wall up to the massive and imposing limestone rock that towers over the town. At the top is the 18th century pilgrimage chapel *Notre-Dame-du-Roc,* and it is worth the exertion for the spectacular view of the entrance to the Verdon Gorge.

FOOD & DRINK

AUBERGE DU TEILLON
Sophisticated restaurant serving regional specialities also on a shaded terrace if preferred. Some 6 km/3.7 mi outside of the town in the direction of Grasse on

The Verdon flows quietly under the Pont du Roc of Castellane, but then it becomes fast and wild

THE HINTERLAND

the Route Napoléon. *Closed Dec–end Feb, otherwise always on Mon | Route Napoléon | tel. 04 92 83 60 88 | www. auberge-teillon.com | Moderate | also 9 rooms | Budget*

WHERE TO STAY

MA PETITE AUBERGE
This hotel, with beautiful gardens and a restaurant with terrace, is located right in the middle of town. *15 rooms | closed Nov–end Feb | Blvd. de la République | tel. 04 92 83 62 06 | www.mapetiteauberge. com | Budget–Moderate | restaurant Moderate | closed Wed, in July, Aug daily*

DU ROC
This basic, but clean and delightful establishment and restaurant is in a central location on Castellane's main square. *10 rooms | Closed Nov | 3, Place de l'Église | tel. 04 92 83 62 65 | hotellerie-du-roc.com | Budget*

INFORMATION

OFFICE DE TOURISME
Rue Nationale | tel. 04 92 83 61 14 | www. castellane.org

WHERE TO GO

GORGES DU VERDON ★
(138–139 C–D2) (*∅ H–J6*)
In prehistory, the river with its source at Sestrière 2800 m/9186 ft above sea level sliced through the limestone rocks of the foothills of the Alpes-de-Haute-Provence like a knife through butter. Today the canyon is one of Europe's largest natural marvels. Steep cliffs on both sides of the gorge have a sheer drop of 700 m/2297 ft. The mountain river with its emerald green water has now been contained by half a dozen dams and is a haven for hikers, extreme climbers and water sports enthusiasts.
Two scenic roads, the *Corniche Sublime* (in the south) and the even more spectacular *Corniche des Crètes* (in the north) offer breathtaking views of the gorge. One such observation point is the 800 m/2625 ft high *Falaise des Cavaliers* (between Comps and Aiguines).
The Gorges du Verdon and surrounds – including the 1000 m/3281 ft high village of *La Palud-sur-Verdon* – is a *Parc Naturel Régional*. Worth a visit is the interesting *Maison des Gorges du Verdon* museum *(mid March–mid Nov 10am–noon and 4pm–6pm | 4 euros | le Château | le Palud sur Verdon | www.lapaludsurverdon. com)*. Information: *Parc Naturel Régional du Verdon (Domaine de Valx | Moustiers-Sainte-Marie | tel. 04 92 74 68 00 | www. parcduverdon.fr)*

MONTAGNE DU CHEIRON (135 E–F 4–5–136 A–B 4–5) (*∅ M–O 5–6*)
The natural valleys and idyllic mountain villages surrounding the 1777 m/5830 ft

Wild water adventures between the rock faces: rafting in the Gorges du Verdon

high peak of the Cheiron mountain –
some 50 km/30 mi east of Castellane –
are fantastic. The *Cascades aux Gorges
du Loup* make a tremendous noise and,
after the Clue de Gréolières, hint at just
what the river gets up to on its way to
the sea: ⚜ It is worth stopping at the
occasional observation point along the
D 3 between Bramafan and Gourdon.
In between magnificent waterfalls like
the *Cascade des Courmes* or the *Saut
du Loup*.

Gréolières (135 F5) *(⚹ N6)* is the hub
of the area and it is from here that
hiking and canyoning excursions to
the Loup and Estéron valleys set out.
Must-see villages are the carefully restored *Coursegoules* (136 A5) *(⚹ N6)*
1000 m/3281 ft up or *Roquestéron-
Grasse* (136 A4) *(⚹ N5)* (65 residents)
with its fortified ⚜ *Sainte-Pétronille*
church dating back to the 12th century
and overlooking the magnificent Estéron
valley. Information on the regional nature reserve is available at the information centre of the *Parc Naturel Régional*
*des Préalpes d'Azur (1, Av. François Goby |
Saint-Vallier-de-Thiey | tel. 04 92 42 39 29 |
www.pnr-prealpesdazur.fr).*

MOUSTIERS-SAINTE-MARIE ★
(138 C1) *(⚹ H5)*

A picture-perfect mountain village ap-
proximately 45 km/28 mi from Castellane nestling at the foot of two massive
rocks not far from the Verdon Gorge. Sus-
pended between the rocks is a silver star
whose legacy goes back to a legend from
the Middle Ages. Moustiers (pop. 700)
was once occupied by the monks of the
Iles de Lérins off Cannes and became an
important centre for faience (tin-glazed
pottery) in the 18th century. After a crisis
in the 19th century, the industry has since
experienced a revival with some 20 manufacturers in business here.

Moustiers has become very chic as ev-
idenced by the opening of Michelin
starred chef Alain Ducasse's restaurant: *La Bastide de Moustiers (Chemin
de Quinson | tel. 04 92 70 47 47 | www.
bastide-moustiers.com | Expensive | also*

12 rooms | *Expensive*). On the church square INSIDER TIP *La Treille Muscate* with its cosy terrace, authentic Provençal cuisine and excellent service also comes recommended (*closed Nov–Jan, closed Wed July/Aug, closed Wed/Thu Feb–Oct | Place de l'Église | tel. 04 92 74 64 31 | www.restaurant-latreillemuscate.fr | Moderate*). Information: *Place de l'Église | tel. 04 92 74 67 84 | www.moustiers.eu*

Moustiers-Sainte-Marie is a good starting point for excursions to the Verdon Gorge or the *Lac de Sainte-Croix*, a dam built in 1975 that offers a whole range of water sports like those in Sainte-Croix or Bauduen, and where you can hire a paddle boat to take you right into the gorge.

QUINSON (138 A3) (*ĴŴ G7*)

This typical Provençal village (pop. 420) on the Verdon river has deliberately embraced the past in order to stay abreast of tourism of the future. Built 75 km/46.6 mi from Castellane at the most southerly end of the *Sainte-Croix* dam, is renowned British architect Sir Norman Foster's ultra-modern museum of prehistory: ★ *Musée de Préhistoire des Gorges du Verdon* (*spring and autumn Wed–Mon 10am–7pm, July and Aug daily 10am–8pm | 7 euros | Route de Montmeyan | www.museeprehistoire.com*).

COTIGNAC

(138 B5) (*ĴŴ H8*) **The South of France is a gourmet's paradise – but Cotignac (pop. 2200) goes even further, staging numerous festivals in summer celebrating, amongst other things, wine, pasta, and honey, each with its own festival. If you don't put on weight here, it's your own fault: no one should ignore the tiny restaurants with terraces under the chestnut trees.**

Artists and musicians are rediscovering the towns of the Haut-Var region halfway between the A 8 and the Sainte-Croix dam. Once known for its tanneries, oil mills and silk spinning mills, nowadays Cotignac becomes a meeting place once a week with its ● INSIDER TIP *Marché Provençal de Cotignac* (*every Tue | Cours Gambetta*).

SIGHTSEEING

OLD TOWN

A walk through the narrow alleyways of old town Cotignac leads to the *Théâtre de la Verdure*, an outdoor theatre where concerts and theatre productions are performed. From the church you can walk to the natural rock caves ⥤ *Grotte de Cotignac* and from here you will have an excellent view across the valley with its vineyards.

FOOD & DRINK

RESTAURANT DU COURS
Lauded by the locals as having the town's best cuisine, this unassuming restaurant with its terrace is popular for its typical home cooked regional fare like quail *(caille)* and rabbit *(lapin)*. *Closed Dec–mid March, Tue and Wed evenings | 18, Cours Gambetta | tel. 04 94 04 78 50 | www.restaurant-hotelducours.fr | Budget*

SHOPPING

Cotignac is renowned for its honey, wine and oil. Good local honey is obtainable at *Ruchers du Bessillon (2, Cours Gambetta | www.lesruchersdubessillon.com).*

WHERE TO STAY

DOMAINE DE NESTUBY
Located on a quiet wine estate just outside town, it has simple, clean guest rooms decorated in the Provençal style. Also has a swimming pool and sauna. *4 rooms | 4540, Route de Monfort | tel. 04 94 04 60 02 | www.nestuby-provence.com | Moderate*

INFORMATION

Pont de la Cassole | tel. 04 94 04 61 87 | www.la-provence-verte.net

WHERE TO GO

ABBAYE DU THORONET ★
(138 C5) *(Ϻ J9)*
The oldest of the Provence's three Cistercian abbeys lies some 20 km/12.4 mi south of Cotignac. Le Thoronet dating back to the 12th century is a Provençal masterpiece of the Romanesque period characterised by simplicity and precision. The building was neglected after the French Revolution and the abbey became derelict. In the 19th century it was rescued from imminent ruin and restored by author and conservationist Prosper Mérimée. The cloister, abbey church and the chapter house are its main showpieces. *April–Sept daily 10am–6.30pm, Oct–March 10am–1pm and 2pm–5pm | 7.50 euros | thoronet.monuments-nationaux.fr*

BARJOLS (138 A4) *(Ϻ G8)*
This charming village (pop. 3000) lies some 13 km/8.1 mi to the west and has about 30 fountains. Take a stroll through the village centre with its landmark 12 m/39.4 ft diameter plane tree on the town hall square. Information: *Blvd. Grisolle | tel. 04 94 77 20 01 | www.la-provence-verte.net*

COMMANDERIE DE PEYRASSOL
(142 C2) *(Ϻ H9)*
All around this 2100-acre wine estate in Flassans-sur-Issole (30 km/18.6 mi south), in the vineyards, olive groves, all around the cellar and the house, gallery owner Valerie Bach has placed over 50 sculptures by French and international artists (such as Niki de Saint Phalle, Anne and Patrick Poirier, Jaume Pensa, Frank Stella, Gloria Friedmann and Carsten Höller). The signposted walks to the major art (illustrated map at the entrance) are free. From the middle of April, guestrooms are available for the duration of the season (*Moderate*), and on reservation a *table d'hôte* (Moderate) in a medieval stone building. *Wine tastings Mon–Sat at 11am, 2.30pm and 5pm | on the DN7 | tel. 04 94 69 71 02 | www.peyrassol.com*

INSIDER TIP ▶ CORRENS ◔
(138 B5) *(Ϻ G8)*
Correns (pop. 800) 4 km/2.5 mi southwest of Cotignac is France's first organic village. The mayor, a winemaker

Plenty of sun, good soil, rain – that's all a good wine needs. According to the organic vintners of Correns

himself, started the trend and the other farmers followed suit. Every year the community has an organic festival. The former luxury hotel *Auberge du Parc (Place Général de Gaulle | tel. 04 94 59 53 52 | www.aubergedecorrens. fr | Moderate | 6 rooms | Moderate)* may be a little more down-to-earth, but it still maintains the swimming pool in the garden and serves the local organic wine. A very nice opportunity to swim in pristine nature can be had at ● **INSIDER TIP** *Vallon Sourn* to the west of Cotignac, an idyllic gorge with rocks to climb that is well shaded by trees. Information: *2, Rue Cabassonne | tel. 04 94 37 21 31 | correns.fr*

ENTRECASTEAUX (138 C5) (*Ø H8*)
The small village (pop. 1000) 8 km/5 mi to the east of Cotignac overlooking the Bresque valley is proud of its imposing 17th century castle, the *Château d'Entrecasteaux (daily tours Easter–Oct 4pm | 7 euros | www.chateau-entrecasteaux.*

com) with its *Jardin public à la Française par le Nôtre* designed by architect André Le Nôtre. *Information: Cours Gabriel Peri | tel. 04 94 59 95 64 | www.tourisme. entrecasteaux.fr*

SALERNES (138 C4) (*Ø H8*)
Salernes (pop. 3700) 12 km/7.5 mi east of Cotignac has been manufacturing the traditional hexagonal red terracotta tiles or *tomettes* for centuries and they are still in demand throughout France. **INSIDER TIP** *Alain Vagh (Route d'Entrecasteaux | tel. 04 94 70 61 85 | www.alain vagh.fr)* uses them to cover cars, boats and even pianos.

The Terra Rossa museum (Wed–Mon March–Nov 10am–6pm and in midsummer until 7pm | 4 euros | Quartier des Launes | terrarossasalernes.over-blog.fr) in a disused factory takes you through the craft's interesting history. Information: *Place Gabriel Péri | tel. 04 94 70 69 02 | www.ville-salernes.fr*

SILLANS-LA-CASCADE
(138 B–C4) (*ሠ H8*)

This lovingly restored village with its 18th century *Château Manoir* lies 6 km/3.7 mi from Cotlgnac. The village got its name from the INSIDER TIP *Chute d'eau à Sillans-la-Cascade*, an impressive 40 m/131.2 ft waterfall and it only takes half an hour on foot to get there. The family-run *Hôtel-Restaurant Les Pins (closed Mon in summer, Mon and Tue in winter | 1, Grande Rue | tel. 04 94 04 63 26 | www.restaurant-lespins. com | Budget–Moderate | also 5 rooms, Budget)* with a fireplace and shady terrace in summer specialises in Provençal cuisine at affordable prices.

VILLECROZE (138 C4) (*ሠ J8*)

The highlights of Villecroze (pop. 1100, 24 km/14.9 mi east) are its medieval arcades and the *Jardin de la cascade*, a park with *waterfall* and a *rose garden* set beneath a hill. *Tours through the grottos July–mid Sept 10am–noon, 2.30pm–7pm, May, June and Easter 2pm–6pm | 2.50 euros | www.mairie-villecroze.com*

ENTREVAUX

(135 E3–4) (*ሠ M5*) **This village seems to consist only of steps: they wind endlessly all over the slope of the old down of Entrevaux (pop. 880). The fold fortress has been retained and is in perfect condition. In bygone days, it was intended to protect against insistent knights of Nice, but today it's well worth the fabulous hike.**

The *Citadel* that looms large above the medieval settlement on the Var was turned into an almost impenetrable fortress by the 17th century engineer Sébastien Le Prestre de Vauban and was on the border between France and the county of Nice until 1860. A speciality of the area is *secca,* dried salted beef served thinly sliced.

SIGHTSEEING

It only takes half an hour to walk up to the *Citadel,* and the 17th century *cathédrale Notre-Dame-de-l'Assomption d'Entrevaux* with its baroque portal is well worth a visit.

WHERE TO STAY

INSIDER TIP LA MAISON DE JULIE

Generously proportioned, beautifully furnished rooms in the tasteful establishment of the Bolgari family in the village of Le Plan, 2 km/1.2 mi from Entrevaux. *3 rooms, 1 apartment | Closed Dec–Mar | Place Sainte-Marguerite | Le Plan d'Entrevaux | tel. 04 93 02 46 42 | www.maisonjulie.com | Budget*

INFORMATION

BUREAU DU TOURISME
Porte Royale | tel. 04 93 05 46 73 | www.entrevaux.info

WHERE TO GO

AIGLUN (135 F5) (*ሠ M5*)

The 25 km/15.5 mi route to the mountain village of Aiglun (pop. 90) offers spectacular views of southern France's two most impressive ravines: *Clue de Riolan* and *Clue d'Aiglun*. The main road runs through an arch to the *Auberge du Calendal* hotel and restaurant *(5 rooms | 1 dormitory | restaurant closed in Feb, Tue evenings, Sun out of season | tel. 04 93 05 82 32 | www.auberge-aiglun.com | Budget).*

INSIDER TIP GORGES DE DALUIS & GORGES DU CIANS
(135 E–F 2–3) (*ሠ M–N4*)

The 7 km/4.4 mi stretch of the *Gorges de Daluis* ravines some 14 km/8.7 mi north-west show the force with which the Var river made its deep cuts through the red rock between Daluis and Guillaumes. Halfway is the bridge *Pont de la Mariée*, where legend has it that a bride plunged to her death. This is also where ings: *Maison de Pays (Puget-Théniers | RN 202 | tel. 04 93 05 05 05 | www.provence-val-dazur.com);* information on Guillaumes: *Médiathèque | 25, Place de Provence | tel. 04 93 05 57 76 | www.pays-de-guillaumes.com*

A piece of the hinterland for your home: you can buy *secca*, dried beef, in Entrevaux

INSIDER TIP *river hikes* and *canyoning excursions* set out from. Excursions must be accompanied by a guide. A staging point for excursions is *Guillaume. Hotel-Restaurant: Les Chaudrons (10 rooms | tel. 04 93 05 50 01 | Budget).*

You can reach the *Gorges du Cians* via the 1669 m/5476 ft high Valberg ski resort or by taking a detour via the village of Péone. The surroundings here are noticeably wilder than in the aforementioned neighbouring ravine. The D 28 winds its way through half a dozen tunnels leading into yet another view of dramatic beauty. Information and tour book-

TRAIN DES PIGNES ★ ●

(135 D–F 3–4) (L–N5)

Take a leisurely trip in an old carriage steam train from Nice to Digne on the spectacular 'pine route'. It runs on weekends from mid May to the end of October and takes an hour and a half to do the trip from Puget-Théniers to Annot. Information: *www.traindespignes.fr | reservations Gare des Chemins de Fer de la Provence (4 bis, Rue Alfred Binet | Nice | tel. 04 97 03 80 80 | www.trainprovence.com)* or *Gare d'Annot (return journey 20 euros | tel. 04 92 83 20 26 | www.annot.com)*

DISCOVERY TOURS

① FRENCH RIVIERA AT A GLANCE

START: ① Menton **END:** ⑮ Toulon	7 days Driving time (without stops) 9 hours
Distance: ➡ 250 km/155 mi	

COSTS: 1000 euros/person for fuel, accommodation, meals and boat trips

WHAT TO PACK: Swimming things, sun protection

IMPORTANT TIPS: In the high season and during events such as the Formula 1 in Monaco or the film festival in Cannes, accommodation prices are often twice what they usually are. In high season, there are often jams and delays on the coastal routes.

Would you like to explore the places that are unique to this region? Then the Discovery Tours are just the thing for you – they include terrific tips for stops worth making, breathtaking places to visit, selected restaurants and fun activities. It's even easier with the Touring App: download the tour with map and route to your smartphone using the QR Code on pages 2/3 or from the website address in the footer below – and you'll never get lost again even when you're offline.

TOURING APP

→ p. 2/3

Elegant seaside resorts, fabulous parks, exceptional themed museums and top gastronomy, but also wonderful landscapes and medieval villages, islands and colourful markets: the route from Menton to Toulon brings you up close to all the facets of the French Riviera.

Before you leave ❶ Menton → p. 37, the town on the Italian borders with its palm trees, the Baroque church of **Saint-Michel-Archange** and the **Jean Cocteau Museum** by the sea, take a stroll around the **Art Nouveau market hall** in the harbour. **Then set off and follow the sea to**

DAY 1

❶ Menton 🏠 🏛 🛍

11 km/6.8 mi

Photo: View of Monaco and the yacht harbour

95

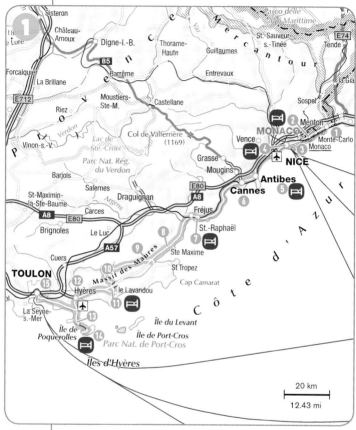

② Monaco

② Monaco → p. 32. For a snack at lunchtime, head for the terrace of the **Oceanographic Museum**, where you can then spend the whole afternoon looking at what the principality is doing for science. Try your luck in the **casino** in the evening, and then enjoy the three-star cuisine at the **Louis XV** next door. And if the big win doesn't happen for you, you can still spend the night at the surprisingly reasonable **Hôtel de France**.

DAY 2

13 km/8.1 mi

③ Cap Ferrat

Follow the coast to ③ Cap Ferrat → p. 49 and visit the **Villa & Jardins Ephrussi de Rothschild**. This building, which was built in the Italian style in 1910, has a INSIDER TIP small café where you can enjoy some refreshment after a walk through the fabulous park with views of the sea. Later in the afternoon, head for ❹ **Nice** → **p. 40**. In recent years, this metropolis in the Bay of Angels has grown more and more into a tourist centre. The **Plage Beau Rivage** right on the beach is ideal for an evening meal in summer, while the **Hôtel Windsor** with rooms designed by various artists is a lovely place to spend the night. Next morning, be sure to visit the big **market** on the **Cours Saleya**, with its colourful flowers and equally colourful foods.

Go via Cagnes-sur-Mer and the coastal route along wonderful sandy beaches – where you'll definitely want to relax for a while – on your way to ❺ **Antibes** → **p. 54**. With the **Musée Picasso** in Chateau Grimaldi right beside the sea, the town is a guarantee for great art. But it's not all Picasso here: it's well worth a stroll through the building to see the Hans Hartung collection, the large hall that is dedicated to Nicolas de Staël, and the terrace with sculptures by Germaine Richier as well. After enjoying the art, take a stroll through the **old town of Antibes**, dine in the eponymous **restaurant** in the **Safranier** quarter, and spend the night a few steps from the beach at the hotel **La Jabotte**.

Stay by the water, and next day drive to ❻ **Cannes** → **p. 58**, and follow in the film stars' footsteps from the **Boulevard de la Croisette** with the **festival bunker** to the brightly coloured **Marché Forville**, where you can enjoy a delicious lunch at **Le Bistrot Gourmand**. **Go via Théoule-sur-Mer** parallel to the blue Mediterranean, through red cliffs and green forests, **along the Corniche de l'Esterel** and stop for a swim at **Camp Long beach** near Agay, then on to ❼ **Saint-Raphaël** → **p. 66**. You would be well advised to dine at the **Brasserie Tradition et Gourmandise**, and then to spend the night at the little hotel **La Chêneraie**.

Next day, **after** ❽ **Sainte-Maxime** → **p. 79 in the Bay of Saint-Tropez**, where cafés and beaches are cheaper and not as busy as they are in the luxury resort opposite, **the road winds up into the hinterland**. With its castle ruins and cork oak forests, ❾ **Grimaud** → **p. 75** is the **stopover on the way to** ❿ **Collobrières** → **p. 74**, where you can stock up on any and all kinds of chestnut specialities. **From there, drive on to the mimosa forests of**

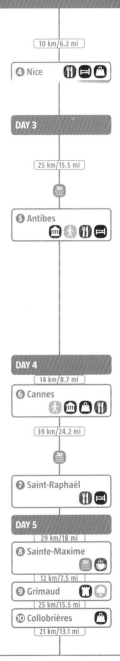

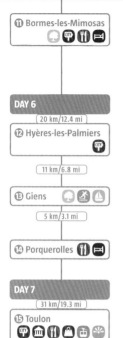

⑪ Bormes-les-Mimosas → p. 74, one of the prettiest villages in France. Immerse yourself in the bustle of the alleys. It's well worth booking a table at the restaurant **Lou Portaou** for dinner, before spending the night at the **Hôtel Bellevue**.

DAY 6

20 km/12.4 mi

⑫ Hyères-les-Palmiers

11 km/6.8 mi

⑬ Giens

5 km/3.1 mi

⑭ Porquerolles

Leave the beaches of Le Lavandou, which was once a part of Bormes-les-Mimosas, to the others, and **drive straight to ⑫ Hyères-les-Palmiers** → p. 71, which even has a reference to its wonderful palm trees in its name. Enjoy a stroll through the pretty **old town** before heading south. The tombolo sandy strip with its salt gardens and the beaches that are so popular with surfers links the former island of **⑬ Giens** → p. 72 with the mainland. Boats head from the *Tour Fondue* to the "Golden Islands" → p. 73 Porquerolles, Port-Cros and Levant. Treat yourself to an evening meal and a bed at the **Mas du Langoustier** on **⑭ Porquerolles**, the largest of the three *Iles d'Or*.

DAY 7

31 km/19.3 mi

⑮ Toulon

Then leave the island and head back to normal life. **The route from Giens via Le Pradet takes you to France's most important military harbour, ⑮ Toulon** → p. 80. The town has shaken off its reputation as a grey mouse by the sea, and with its harbour promenade, old town markets, museums and restaurants, is definitely worth visiting. At the end of your trip, don't forget to take the cable car up **Mont Faron**, where you can admire the Bay of Toulon in all its glory.

2

THE LAND OF FRAGRANCE

START: ① Antibes	3 days
END: ① Antibes	Driving time
	(without stops)
Distance:	2.5 hours
🚗 100 km/62 mi	

COSTS: approx. 350 euros/person for accommodation, meals, admissions and fuel

WHAT TO PACK: Comfortable shoes for walking around villages and towns

IMPORTANT TIPS: The old towns of Saint-Paul-de-Vence and Mougins are closed to traffic. In Grasse, it's a good idea to head straight to the central multi-storey car park.

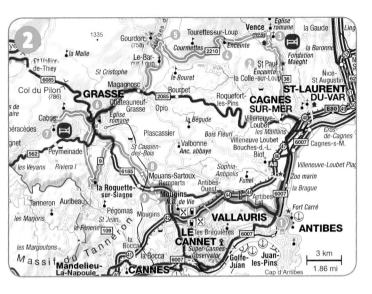

Roses and violets, oranges and lemons, gorse and mimosa. The area around Grasse is the land of fragrances and aroma, and the town itself the middle of a route that in three days offers you all the contrasts that make up the French Riviera as if under a microscope. Commit all your senses to this abundance and variety: sniff all the flacons, taste the candied Seville oranges, immerse yourself in modern art, and enjoy the feeling of the southern sun on your skin.

This view when you start in ➊ Antibes → p. 54 of the fortress wall near the Musée Picasso in the old Chateau Grimaldi will simply overwhelm you: the blue sea of the Bay of Angels, next to it the futuristic, pyramid- shaped holiday resort Marina Baie des Anges of 1970, followed by the nice silhouette of Nice, and above it all the peaks of the Maritime Alps.

Continue via Cagnes-sur-Mer on the D 2 north to ➋ **Saint-Paul-de-Vence** → p. 53 with the **Fondation Maeght**, one of the best-known places of pilgrimage for followers of modern art. Before the visit, it's a good idea to take a stroll around the village with its tiny cafés, many galleries and the world-famous restaurant **La Colombe d'Or**. It's only a stone's throw to ➌ **Vence** → p. 51 and the basic but pleasant guesthouse **La Lubiane** for the night. Enjoy some retail therapy in the pretty shops that line the alleys in the **old town**.

DAY 1

➊ Antibes

19 km/11.8 mi

➋ Saint-Paul-de-Vence

9 km/5.6 mi

➌ Vence

A rose by any other name: harvesting rose petals for perfume at Grasse

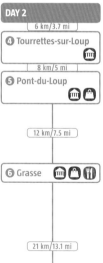

DAY 2

6 km/3.7 mi

④ Tourrettes-sur-Loup 🏛

8 km/5 mi

⑤ Pont-du-Loup 🏛 🛍

12 km/7.5 mi

⑥ Grasse 🏛 🛍 🍽

21 km/13.1 mi

As you head west from Vence, the landscape on the D 2210 becomes wildly romantic. The route takes you to ④ Tourrettes-sur-Loup**,** the violet metropolis that has a lovely old town. It's worth making a stop at the bridge over the river that was blown up by the Germans in 1944 in ⑤ Pont-du-Loup: the INSIDER **TIP** Confiserie Florian *(daily 9am–6.30pm in summer, otherwise 9am–noon, 2pm–6.30pm | free entrance | guided tours as well | www.confiseriflorian.com)* demonstrates how clever hands can turn tiny violets, rose petals and fruits of the south into jams, sweets and other southern delights. Naturally, you are welcome to sample their wares. Keep the afternoon free for ⑥ Grasse → p. 62, the fragrance capital since the 17th century. Go and see just what the perfume industry conjures up from flowers and herbs. At the International Perfume Museum, for instance, which is well worth a visit (and a sniff). You can also book a *workshop* at Galimard → p. 64 and create your own perfume. An evening menu of local specialities is on offer at Le Moulin du Sault *(closed Mon, Wed evening, Sun evening | Chemin du Vieux Moulin | Auribeau-sur-Siagne | tel. 04 93 42 25 42 | www. moulindusault.com | Moderate–Expensive)* in a former olive mill **just 5 km/3.1 mi south**

of **Grasse**. For your night's accommodation, drive up to the village of ➐ **Cabris**, where you will find the pretty **Auberge du Vieux Château** → p. 64.

You'll find a little less charm in ➑ **Mouans-Sartoux on the way back south**, but apart from the medieval triangular castle, the little town does have another bright green triumph of the 21st century: the Swiss artists Sybil Albers and Gottfried Honegger left their town their unique collection of art, which includes works by Daniel Buren, Max Bill, Joseph Beuys, Yves Klein, Imi Knoebel, Ulrich Rückriem and Georg Karl Pfahler. For it, the Zurich architects Annette Gigon and Mike Guyon built (and painted green) a 26-m/85.3-ft high INSIDERTIP **museum tower** (**Espace de l'Art Concret**) *(Château de Mouans | Wed–Sun 11am– 6pm, in high summer daily from 11am–7pm | 7 euros | www.es pacedelartconcret.fr)*. Just a few miles along is picture-book pretty ➒ **Mougins** → p. 62, which has golf courses, galleries and the **Museum of Photography** → p. 61 that is dedicated to Pablo Picasso to make it perfect for a visit. The exquisite finishing touch to the tour is waiting in the form of a meal at the **L'Amandier** in Mougins, where your palette will be able to enjoy the aromas and delights of the south one last time. **Follow the D 35 away from the land of fragrances and gourmets, to** ➊ **Antibes** → p. 54 and the sea.

➐ Cabris

DAY 3

13 km/8.1 mi

➑ Mouans-Sartoux

4 km/2.5 mi

➒ Mougins

15 km/9.3 mi

➊ Antibes

COASTAL WALK ALONG THE PENINSULA OF SAINT-TROPEZ

START: ➊ Plage de Gigaro
END: ➊ Plage de Gigaro

approx. 6 hours, walking time (without stops) 4 hours

Distance: easy
🔄 14 km/8.7 mi 📶
Altitude: 250 m/850 ft

COSTS: approx. 25 euros/person for parking and a picnic
WHAT TO PACK: Sensible shoes, swimming things, sun protection, plenty of water and food

IMPORTANT TIPS: Part of the walk takes you over rough and smooth, as well as smooth rocks. Because the path is often damaged by heavy breakers, especially in winter, contact the Tourist Office first for information on its condition.

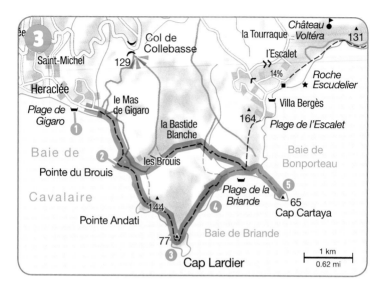

Bathing on the peninsula of Saint-Tropez on a deserted beach in the middle of summer? The *sentier littoral* → p. 22, the 19-km/11.8-mi coastal hiking trail (marked in yellow) from Cavalaire to Cap Camarat makes it possible, and is an amazing experience at any time of the year. It's almost impossible to finish the entire route in one day, but you could manage the section from the Plage de Gigaro in La-Croix-Valmer to Cap Taillat, there and back and including swimming stops, in 6 hours.

The coastal path is an achievement of the *Conservatoire du Littoral*, which was founded in 1975 and not only vehemently opposes residential developments on the coast, but also cares for the flora and fauna and repairs the hiking path when necessary, whenever it is damaged by exceptionally high waves. **The starting point for the hiking trail with views of the sky and sea is the ❶ Plage de Gigaro**, where – with a little luck – you will also find somewhere to park (for a fee) in the middle of summer. The roughly 700-acre coastal strip from Mas du Gigaro to the Cap Taillat peninsula is a protected area that is open to the public. The cliff with the aleppo pines and cork oak forests is a haven for blackbirds, green woodpeckers, sparrows and seagulls.

On the easy route from the Plage de Gigaro to ❷ Pointe du Brouis you will notice how the number of towels on the beach dwindles even within half an hour. You'll be almost entirely alone in the next bay, so you can enjoy your picnic in peace and your first dip in the clear water. Refreshed and fortified, follow the exemplary signage on the path in the shade of the trees and accompanied by the fragrance of spicy herbs, past the lighthouse and **up to ❸ Cap Lardier**. There, from the southern tip of the peninsula of Saint-Tropez, enjoy the fabulous views of the sea **before then setting off over rough and smooth along the hiking trail, past small bays that are deserted even in the middle of summer, to the ❹ Baie de Briande**, where the most you might spot could be a couple of sailing boats at anchor.

Stay beside the sea, cross the wide beach of the Bastide Blanche, and on the peninsula ❺ INSIDER TIP **Cap Taillat** you will have the choice of sand or rocks for your next leisurely dip. The boats and yachts that congregate here on trips from Saint-Tropez usually stay a polite distance from the beach. **For the route back to Gigaro beach, take the shortcut across the vineyard of the Bastide Blanche**, which belongs to the Domaine de la Croix but cannot be visited, through the forests with the *pins parasol*, the pines that open out their green roof of needles like sun umbrellas, and fields that demonstrate that agriculture does indeed

2,4 km/1.5 mi

❸ Cap Lardier

1,5 km/0.9 mi

❹ Baie de Briande

1,6 km/1 mi

❺ Cap Taillat

6,2 km/3.9 mi

"Oh, how lovely!": the *sentier littoral* offers fabulous views after every turn

still have a future, even here in this paradise of the jet-set. **You are already familiar with the beach at the Pointe du Brouis, and at ① Plage de Gigaro** you'll be back in civilisation and ready to enjoy an evening meal beside the sea at the restaurant **Couleurs Jardin** (daily April–Sep | tel. 04 94 79 59 12 | www.restaurantcouleursjardin.com | *Moderate*).

① Plage de Gigaro

4 LEISURE SPORTS IN THE ROYA VALLEY

START: ① Menton	3 days
END: ① Menton	Driving time
	(without stops)
Distance:	3 hours
🚗 125 km/78 mi	

COSTS: 300 euros/person for accommodations, meals, fuel and toll charges in Italy

WHAT TO PACK: Hiking boots for excursions into the mountains, equipment for kayaking or canyoning, warm clothing even in summer

IMPORTANT TIP: The narrow road from Breil-sur-Roya to Tende has been under development for years. There are constant roadworks that can cause long jams.

Even at the height of summer, a trip from Menton into the valley of the Roya will cool you down. The hinterland of the French Riviera awakes. The valley has developed the infrastructure for sporting offers. Kayaking, canyoning, hiking in the national park or climbing on a *via ferrata* – the possibilities here are tremendous. From Menton, go through Sospel to get to the Roya valley and return via Ventimiglia in Italy.

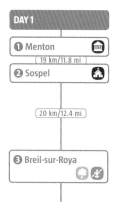

DAY 1

① Menton 🏛

19 km/11.8 mi

② Sospel 🏠

20 km/12.4 mi

③ Breil-sur-Roya

From ① Menton → p. 37, **the winding D 2566 takes you through the Vallée du Caraï to ② Sospel.** The major landmark in the second-biggest city in the county of Nice, is the 15th century bridge, once a toll-gate on the *Route du Sel*, the salt route. It was destroyed in WWII, and rebuilt in 1953 using stones from the bed of the Bévéra river. The cathedral of **Saint Michel** on a square surrounded by medieval tiled houses is worth a visit. **From Sospel, the D 2204 takes you via the Col de Brouis (879 m/2884 ft) to the banks of the Roya.**

The starting point for your sporting trip is ③ **Breil-sur-Roya.** The village is situated on both banks of the mountain river, which here has been dammed to make an artificial lake. The local Office du Tourisme *(Place Biancheri | tel. 04 93 04 99 76 | www.breil-sur-roya.fr)* will provide you with details of kayaking courses and canyoning excursions into the region's wonderful gorges. Why not just give it a go! **A little further up-river is ④ Saorge → p. 84**, one of the prettiest rock villages in France. The guesthouse **Ca'Da Barrera** *(5 rooms | 1, Rue Doumergue | tel. 06 16 44 08 26 | www.chambres dhotes-saorge.fr | Moderate)* will also provide you with an evening meal by prior agreement *(Budget)*.

From Saorge, you can enjoy some wonderful walks through the Mercantour National Park → p. 83 on the next day. **Then continue driving north.** You will definitely enjoy a night at the hotel restaurant **Le Mirval** *(18 rooms | closed Oct–April | 3, Rue Vincent Ferrier | tel. 04 93 04 63 71 | www.lemirval.com | Budget)* in **⑤ La Brigue**. In the past, the village has belonged to the Provence, to Savoyen, to France, to the Piedmont and to Italy, and in 1947 was returned to France, along with the Roya valley, following a referendum. Its 600 residents are proud to have no fewer than **INSIDER TIP seven historical monuments**. A 90-minute stroll will take you to the tiny chapels that have been built around the village over the course of the centuries. If you're of a more sporty inclination, you can hike up **Mont Bertrand** (2483 m/8146 ft) in a good 5 hours.

The last day is really exciting. The latest thing for an adventure in the Maritime Alps is what is known as a *via ferrata*, the Italian name for a hiking trail of dizzying heights that are fully fitted out with crampons, ladders, walkways and bridges. You can book and try one in the mountain village of **⑥ Tende**, where the walkway (20 m/65.6 ft long and 40 cm/1.3 ft wide) between two rocks can be seen from far off as the highlight of the **Via ferrata des Comtes Lascaris** *(www.tendemerveilles.com)*. Back in Tende, the **Musée des Merveilles → p. 85** is perfect for pleasant, entertaining break after so much

| 45 km/28 mi |
| **7** Ventimiglia |
| 10 km/6.2 mi |
| **1** Menton |

activity. **On the coast, the fastest way from Breil-sur-Roya is via the French D 6204 to the border, then the Italian SR 20 via 7 Ventimiglia**, with its (compared with France) cheap shopping and large market. **Follow the coast and the Via Aurelia back to France and 1 Menton** → p. 37.

5 FROM GORGE TO GORGE IN THE HINTERLAND

START:	**1** Puget-Théniers	3 days
END:	**11** Moustiers-Sainte-Marie	Driving time
Distance:		(without stops)
→ 190 km/118 mi		3½ hours

COSTS: Approx. 250 euros/person plus fuel plus 20 euros for the Pine Cone Train
WHAT TO PACK: Good shoes for walks and lookout points

IMPORTANT TIPS: Take great care on the narrow roads along the gorges, especially on the Route des Crêtes in the Verdon. Outside the high season in summer, many of the restaurants in the hinterland are closed, but you'll be welcome in Moustiers-Sainte-Marie all year round.

The hinterland of the French Riviera has preserved its dry charm, and offers fabulous landscapes with gorges that were carved into the mountains by rivers such as the Var or the Verdon. This tour will take you along to the mountain world, about 100 km/62 mi from the Mediterranean. The Gorges de Daluis or Gorges du Verdon, also known as the Grand Canyon, are a paradise for hikers and active people. Valberg even has its own ski station with a wellness spa and lovely hiking trails. Entrevaux and Moustiers-Sainte-Marie are two of the prettiest villages in France, and have a culinary offer that leaves practically nothing to be desired.

DAY 1

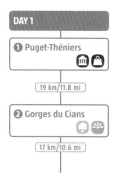

| **1** Puget-Théniers |
| 19 km/11.8 mi |
| **2** Gorges du Cians |
| 17 km/10.6 mi |

The starting point for the tour is the little town of **1 Puget-Théniers** north-west of Nice on the banks of the Var river; the Maison de Pays *(www.provence-val-dazur.com)* houses the tourism centre of the regional nature reserve. You can also stock up on the region's specialities such as liqueurs and jams here. **Then take the D 6202 east. In Le Pont du Cians turn onto the D 28 heading north, and you'll instantly be in the 2 Gorges du Cians**, the gorges of the River Cian, which has its source in the Mercantour National Park. The spectacular road through the red cliffs **goes though the medieval** village of Beuil and to the modern tourist centre ❸ **Val-berg**, appealing to sporty people all year round. Take the chair lift up to the **Croix du Sapet**, and enjoy INSIDER TIP ab-seiling through the tree tops and back down to the **station (Espace Valberg Aventure)** *(daily in high summer | 14–23 euros, depending on the course)*. For an inexpensive lunch and coffee, go to the Restaurant **Les Terrasses du Soleil** *(Av. Saint-Bernard | tel. 04 93 02 60 73 | Budget)*.

Fortified, head on to **Guillaumes** and the entrance to the ❹ **Gorges de Daluis** → p. 92. At the end of the village is the **Pont de la Mariée** with the first panoramic views of the gorge, a breathtaking natural spectacle on the D 2202. **At the end of the gorge, drive a short distance back to** ❺ **Entrevaux** → p. 92, where you will find one of the loveliest guestrooms in the region at **La Maison de Julie**.

After the lavish breakfast with regional fruit juices and home-made jam, visit Entrevaux with its **citadel** (30-minute walk), and at the weekend enjoy the **Train des**

❸ Valberg

19 km/11.8 mi

❹ Gorges de Daluis

20 km/12.4 mi

❺ Entrevaux

DAY 2

The river offers spectacular gorges and loops, and Entrevaux adapts to them

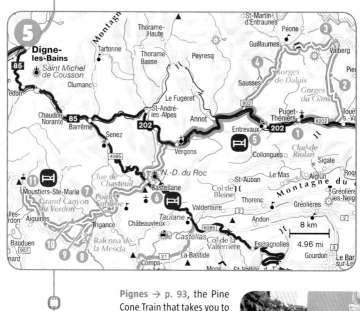

5 Digne-les-Bains

40 km/24.9 mi

6 Castellane
🏰 👣 ❄ 🍴 🛏

DAY 3

16 km/9.9 mi

7 Gorges du Verdon
🌳

2 km/1.2 mi

8 Belvedère du Couloir Samson
❄

14 km/8.7 mi

Pignes → p. 93, the Pine Cone Train that takes you to Annot and back in old carriages pulled by a steam engine. **Take the D 4202 and D 955 to the Verdon valley at 6 Castellane** → **p. 86**. If you still have the energy, walk the 15 minutes up the 184 m/604 ft **Roc**, the cliff above the village that is crowned by the chapel **Notre-Dame-du-Roc**. Dinner and your night's accommodation at the **Ma Petite Auberge** can wait a little while.

The next day takes you deep into the **7 Gorges du Verdon** → **p. 87**. Be sure to stop at the lookout point **8 Belvedère du Couloir Samson**. Enjoy the drive along the narrow road, and don't miss the **hard left turn after 22 km/13.7 mi onto the D 23** to experience the ⑨ **Corniche des Crètes** → p. 87 with breathtaking views from the road of the famous climbing rocks high above the emerald green river. After this bow, you will come to ⑩ **La Palud-sur-Verdon** → p. 87, the tiny capital of the gorges with cafés where the Verdon adventurers meet. **On the way to Moustiers-Sainte-Marie treat yourself to a dip and a break at the beach beside the Pont du Galetas** on Lac de Sainte-Croix. The wonderful village of ⑪ **Moustiers-Sainte-Marie** → p. 88, famous for its Fayence art, has lots of shops with Provençal specialities and crafts, as well as restaurants such as **La Grignotière** *(closed Nov–Mar | Rue de Sainte-Anne | tel. 04 92 74 69 12 | Budget)* with its shady terrace under centuries-old olive trees. Spend the night before you return to the coast in this pretty village. **Maguy Caffort** has two basic but delightful INSIDER TIP guestrooms → p. 89 next to Moustiers' former laundry that are open all year round.

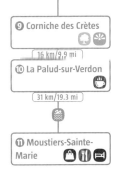

⑨ Corniche des Crètes

16 km/9.9 mi

⑩ La Palud-sur-Verdon

31 km/19.3 mi

⑪ Moustiers-Sainte-Marie

Back to civilisation after the wild gorge: Moustiers-Sainte-Marie has plenty of shops, bars and restaurants

SPORTS & ACTIVITIES

Raging rivers rushing through deep valleys, rugged snow-capped mountains, azure blue sea, beautiful islands as well as uninhabited landscapes and golf courses with fantastic sea views: the French Riviera and its hinterland is ideal for all kinds of sportive activities and wellness.

Amateurs and professionals alike – be they water sports enthusiasts, nature loving hikers, adventure enthusiasts, keen golfers or fearless scuba divers – all get their money's worth here.

Nice's OTC *(Office du Tourisme)* is the best port of call for information on sports and activities on the coast and in the hinterland. Have a look at *www.cotedazur-tourisme.com* and *www.tourismepaca.fr/welcome*

CANYONING

An adventure sport that includes a bit of everything; swimming, running, jumping, abseiling, climbing and even diving. The hinterland is perfect for those wanting to cross ravines along a rope, wade through rivers, and clamber down steep narrow canyons and negotiate active waterfalls. Excursions can last anything from an hour to several days and are all accompanied by an experienced guide. The most popular are the Verdon Gorge and Roya excursions. Irrespective of whether you are a beginner or more advanced the Estéron valley in Aiglun with its *Clue des Mujouls, Clue de Saint-Auban* and *Clue d'Aiglun* provide exceptional canyoning. Obtain advice for this activity in the Verdon region from:

Photo: Boats at the entrance of the great Verdon Gorge

The sea, the beaches, the mountains, rivers and canyons: the French Riviera is an exciting destination for sport and outdoor enthusiasts

Maison des Alpes de Haute-Provence (see p. 124) or in the French brochure *Descente de Canyons dans les Alpes de Haute Provence* by B. Gorgeon. Information on canyoning in the Département Alpes-Maritimes: *Conseil Général 06* (*Nice | www. randoxygene.org)*, which publishes the *Clues et Canyons* tour guide.

CLIMBING

The Verdon Gorge is a popular destination for Europe's extreme climbers.

Just under a thousand climbs of varying degrees of difficulty have been set up in the canyon cliffs. The *Falaise de l'Escalès*, a 300 m/985 ft high vertical cliff face has gained cult status among the climbing fraternity. The chalk rocks of *Annot* or the red cliff faces in *Roquebrune-sur-Argens* are ideal for both beginners and more advanced climbers. For a foretaste of the higher mountain ranges try the cliff faces in the upper *Vallée du Var*. Information on the Verdon Gorge: *Maison des Alpes de*

Haute-Provence (see p. 124). Information on the Maritime Alps: *Comité Régional du Tourisme Riviera-Côte d'Azur* (see p. 124).

Using the iron ladders, railings and rungs on the mountain tracks of the *Vie Ferrate* you can combine mountaineering, climbing and hiking. With very little training but using the professional gear provided, you can climb up steep rocks to dizzying heights and not give crossing the ravine by a rope bridge *Pont de Singe*, a second thought. The INSIDER TIP *Via Ferrata du Baou de la Frema (www.colmiane.com)* in Colmiane-Valdeblore is ideal for beginners whereas the *Via Ferrata des Comtes Lascaris* in Tende will take you to the historical beginnings of the mountain village on the border to Italy. Peille and Puget-Théniers also have newly established climbing trails. Information can be obtained at the local tourist office or from the *Comité Régional du Tourisme Riviera-Côte d'Azur* (see p. 124)

HIKING

The paths once used by the customs officials have undergone a renaissance and are now hiking trails or *sentier littoral* (see p. 22). You can obtain tips and maps in the local tourism offices or from the French hiking association *Fédération Française de la Randonnée Pédestre (64, Rue du Dessous des Berges | Paris | tel. 01 44 89 93 90 | www. ffrandonnee.fr)*. Tips for tours at the Département Alpes-Maritimes, such as the 10 km/6.2 mi INSIDER TIP *sentier planétaire (Planet path; easy to complete in 5 hours)* in Valberg with an altitude difference of 300 m/984 ft and planet sculptures from the sun to Neptune, are available at *www.rand oxygene.org* in the Internet.

SAILING, STAND-UP PADDLING & SURFING

Seven harbours with more than a 1000 moorings lie along the French Riviera coast: Hyères, La Londe, Le Lavandou, Saint-Raphaël, Cannes, Saint-Laurent-du-Var and Antibes. For more information contact: *Fédération Française de Voile (17, rue Henri Bocquillon | 75015 Paris | www.ffvoile.fr)* or the *Stations Nautiques (17, Rue Henri Bocquillon | 75015 Paris | www.station-nautique.com)*.

Mandelieu is one of the French Riviera's most popular year round kite surfing centres, with e.g. *Air'X Kite (Centre Nautique de Mandelieu | Av. du Général de Gaulle | www.airxkite.com)*, but they are also a familiar sight on the beaches of Nice and Toulon. Wind surfers meet up from Easter onwards at the stretch of water – the *tombolo* – that joins the Giens peninsula to Hyères to take advantage of the easterly winds on Bergerie beach in the east and the north-westerly mistral on Almanarre beach in the west.

Friends of stand-up paddling may well find their paradise on the *Plage Du Mouré Rouge (charge for board and paddle 12 euros/hour | www.cannesstanduppaddle.fr)* in Cannes. An overview of other places to paddle on the French Riviera such as Théoule-sur-Mer or Saint-Laurent-du-Var is available from *Yumping (www.yump ing.fr/paddle-surf/alpes-maritimes)*.

SCUBA DIVING & SNORKELLING

A rocky coastline, crystal clear water and a wealth of fish all lure scuba divers and snorkellers to the French Riviera. Just off the island of *Port-Cros* there is the INSIDER TIP *Sentier Sous-marin Port-Cros (Bureau d'Informations du Parc | Port-Cros | tel. 04 94 01 40 72)*, a man-made underwater trail for snorkelling. Scuba divers will be in their element on the rocky coastlines of the Giens and Saint-Tropez peninsula, off the shore at La Napoule, Cannes and Saint-Raphaël. Off the Estérel coast, dozens of intriguing ship and aeroplane wrecks lie on the ocean floor, some just 20 m/65.6 ft below the water surface. Information on some 140 local scuba diving schools can be obtained via the *Fédération Française d'Etudes et de Sports Sous-Marins (24, Quai de Rive-Neuve | Marseille | tel. 04 91 33 99 31)*. Information in English can be found at *www.europeandiving.com*.

WELLNESS

Sea water has healing power – something the French have known since the 19th century. Today, they are the world's biggest providers of thalassotherapy. Although there are no healing spas on the French Riviera, the state-of-the-art thalasso centres in Monaco, Antibes and Cannes provide virtually anything you could ask for. Today, almost every 4-star hotel on the coast also has a wellness or spa area with bathing fun and massages. For information contact the *Comité Régional du Tourisme Riviera – Côte d'Azur* at *www.cotedazur-tourisme.com*.

ZIP SLIDE

Do you dream of flying? So that your cheeks wobble and you tummy turns somersaults? La Colmiane, a good hour north of Nice, has France's longest *zip slide (tel. 06 85 72 62 47 | www.colmiane.com)*. You are attached to the line by a hip strap, and then you whizz down. For 2.5 km/1.6 mi – and bold users can reach speeds of up to 130 km/h/80 mph. For fun on this level, you have to book in advance and expect to pay quite a charge: 35 euros per person.

Get sensational sights on the Verdon River from a mountain wall

TRAVEL WITH KIDS

For children, the Mediterranean Sea is a single massive leisure pool: gentle waves rolling onto fine beaches and rocks that are full of all kinds of fascinating sea creatures. If you need an alternative to the beach, there are also plenty of adventure parks, zoos and – for rainy days – unusual museums.

But it is not only the coast that caters for the smaller customer: the hinterland also offers plenty of fun and water sports on its rivers and lakes.

MONACO AND SURROUNDS

JARDIN ANIMALIER MONACO
(137 D6) (*M P6*)

Monkeys, snakes and jaguars are some of the main attractions at this exotic zoo, which is located on the steep slope above the village of Fontvieille. *Daily 10am–noon, 2pm–5pm, in summer 9am–noon, 2pm–7pm | 5 euros, children 3 euros*

MUSÉE OCÉANOGRAPHIQUE
(137 D6) (*M P6*)

Look at the size of that: a 20 m/65.6 ft long skeleton of a finback whale is on display at the oceanographic museum! Additionally, and in the stunning aquarium the various fish behind the thick glass panes seem close enough to touch. *April–Sept daily 9.30am–7pm, July/Aug until 7.30pm, in winter 10am–6pm | 14 euros, children 7 euros | 2, Av. Saint-Martin | www.oceano.mc*

On land and water:
The best idea for a family holiday on the
French Riviera – from exciting to relaxing

FOUNTAINS ON THE COULÉE VERTE

Nice is usually hot enough for dripping wet feet: you don't have to pay for the bathing fun that is to be had under the splashing fountains of the Coulée Verte, the new park on the central *Place Masséna*.

PARC PHOENIX (141 E3) (*ω O7*)

A welcome break from spending days on the beach, this botanical garden boasts one of Europe's largest greenhouses.

On display are exotic birds, animals and plants. *Daily 9.30am–7.30pm, in winter until 6pm | 3 euros, free entrance for children up to 12 years | 405, Promenade des Anglais*

PITCHOUN FOREST (141 D3) (*ω O7*)

Pitchoun is the French word for 'little child'. Children aged from three to ten have the starring role in this adventure park: it has bridges, tree trunks and branches in a real forest. None of the equipment is higher than 4 m/13.1 ft and safety is a priority. *Mid Feb–mid Nov, July/Aug 10am–5pm daily, otherwise Sat, Sun and during the French school holidays 10am–4pm | 15 euros | 2559, Route de Grasse | Villeneuve-Loubet | www.pitchounforest.com*

CANNES AND SURROUNDS

CAROUSELS IN CANNES

While their parents watch out for stars on the *Croisette*, children enjoy themselves on the old-fashioned carousels *Le Carousssel 1900* and *Cannes 2000*. Right next to the Film Palace, open all year round. *3 euros per ride*

VISIOBULLE (141 D4) (*m̂ O8*)

A boat trip is a treat for any child but this excursion around Cap d'Antibes takes it up a notch. The specially designed glass bottom boat makes this one of the best ways for them to explore the local sea life. *July/Aug 9.25am, 10.40am, 11.55am, 2pm, 3.25pm, 4.50pm, 6.50pm, April–Sept 11am, 1.30pm, 3pm, 4.30pm | 14 euros, children 7 euros | Blvd. Charles Guillaumont | opposite the Office de Tourisme | Juan-les-Pins | www.visiobulle.com*

THE WEST COAST

AQUALAND FRÉJUS (140 A6) (*m̂ L9*)

A nice change from the sea and sand, this aquatic park located on the RN 98 near Fréjus, is one of the region's largest water parks. *June–Sept daily 10am–6pm July/Aug until 7pm | 27 euros, children from 5–10 years 19.50 euros, from 3–4 years 10 euros | www.aqualand.fr*

FRÉJUS SAFARI PARK

(140 A5) (*m̂ L8*)

5 km/3.1 mi north of the city this park is home to big cats, elephants and monkeys as well as flamingos, vultures and

parrots. *Daily 10am–5pm, in summer until 6pm | 16 euros, children aged 9 and under 11.50 euros | www.zoo-frejus.com*

JARDIN OLBIUS-RIQUIER

(142 C5) (*m̂ H11*)

This 17 acre park was once a branch of the Paris institute *Jardin d'Acclimatation* but since 1868 it has belonged to the city of Hyères. Palms, banana trees, cacti and fragrant flowers grow around a small lake and there are plenty of exotic birds. There is a children's playground, a pony club, a cafeteria and a mini zoo. *Daily 7.30am–8pm, in winter until 5.30pm | free entrance | Av. Ambroise Thomas | www.ville-hyeres.fr*

VILLAGE DES TORTUES GONFARON

(142 C3) (*m̂ J10*)

This is a conservation project at the foot of the Massif des Maures and is home to hundreds of freely roaming Hermann tortoises. *March–end Nov daily 9am–7pm | 12 euros, children from 5–16*

years 8 euros | 2 km/1.2 mi outside the village of Gonfaron on the D 75 | www.villagetortues.com

THE HINTERLAND

CANOEING IN BREIL-SUR-ROYA
(137 E4) (*Ø Q5*)
The wild waters of the Roya river are dammed at Breil-sur-Roya – an ideal spot for children to learn to canoe. Information: *Office du Tourisme (Place Biancheri | tel. 04 93 04 99 76 | www.breil-sur-roya.fr)*

COLMIANE FOREST (136 B2) (*Ø O4*)
This fun filled adventure park in Colmiane-Valdeblore near the *via ferrata* offers various courses and 30 different rock climbing exercises. Kids 5 years and older are catered for with a special course. *In summer daily 9am–5pm | children from 3–6 years 10 euros, from 7–12 years 17 euros, older 22 euros | www.colmiane.com*

KAYAKING ON THE VERDON
(138 C2) (*Ø H6*)
At the exit to the gorge in Moustiers-Sainte-Marie and at the Sainte-Croix dam the water sport centre *3lution Voile* offers kayaking courses for beginners and children. Information: *Maison des Alpes de Haute-Provence (see p. 124).* Information on hiring a paddle boat or canoe (from approx. 7 euros per hour): *MYC Plage (May–Sept Plage du Galetas | tel. 04 94 70 22 28)*, *La Cadeno (Club Nautique Saint-Saturnin | Moustiers-Sainte-Marie | tel. 04 92 74 60 85 | lacadeno.free.fr)*

WOLF PARK ALPHA (128 C2) (*Ø O*)
In the Parc National du Mercantour everything revolves around wolves, and there is a fun 1200 m/0.75 mi hiking trail that goes through the nature reserve – *Le Boréon Saint-Martin-Vésubie (summer daily 10am–6pm, otherwise Wed, Sat, Sun 10am–5pm, closed Nov–Christmas | 10 euros, children from 4–12 years 8 euros | www.alpha-loup.com*

Refreshment in sight! You can swim in the Lac de Sainte-Croix. Or go for boat rides

FESTIVALS & EVENTS

In the summer there are festivals back to back, spring is heralded in February with an extravagant display of colour, and by the autumn and winter folk festivals celebrating good food and nature's abundance give the sleepy towns of the hinterland a new lease on life.

FESTIVALS & EVENTS

JANUARY

Rallye Monte-Carlo: the start of this prestigious rally has marked the opening of the motorsports year since 1911

Fête de Saint-Marcel in Barjols: festival in the Haut-Var hinterland honouring Saint Marcel with music, a procession and mass. Since the 14th century it has been a tradition to sacrifice an ox on the weekend closest to 16 January

Festival du Cirque in Monaco: A weeklong festival organised by the principality, it has the world's best acrobats and clowns under one big top tent

FEBRUARY

INSIDER TIP *Fête du Mimosa in Bormes-les-Mimosas:* The village marks the beginning of spring by celebrating its mimosas with a flower parade and festival on the third Sunday of February

Fête du Mimosa in Mandelieu-La-Napoule: A ten-day folk festival of parades and excursions into the mimosa forest

Nice Carnival: For three weeks in February – daily flower parades, street theatre and a huge techno party

La Fête du Citron in Menton: For three whole weeks it's all about oranges and lemons with flower parades, floats and balls – and 200,000 visitors

MARCH/APRIL

Windsurf World Cup in Hyères: Beginning of March on both the beaches between Hyères and the Giens peninsula

MAY/JUNE

Cannes Film Festival: The world's most prestigious film festival held here every May since 1946

Monaco Grand Prix: Formula One's only race through the streets of a city

Bravade de Saint-Tropez: Procession and festival in mid May in honour of the city's patron saint

Midem in Cannes: The world's biggest music fair at the beginning of June – at the Festival House, but mainly on the streets and in the bars. Amy Winehouse was discovered here

A lively mix of festivals, fairs, carnivals and Formula One makes the French Riviera's calendar of events quite unique

Bravade des Espagnol de Saint-Tropez: A festival held on 15 June to commemorate the victory over the Spanish fleet in 1637

JULY

Jazz à Juan: An international jazz festival staged in the Juan-les-Pins forest.
Nice Jazz Festival: Only a stone's throw from the beach, the Jardin Albert 1 hosts the world's jazz greats.

AUGUST

Fête du Jasmin in Grasse: Beginning of August the town celebrates this fragrant flower with parades and floats

SEPTEMBER/OCTOBER

Monaco Yacht Show: As a real spectator magnet, this fair showcases Europe's luxury super yachts
Les Voiles de Saint-Tropez: Regatta in the gulf of Saint-Tropez at the beginning of the month

DECEMBER

Lucéram's 'Circuit des Crèches': Christmas is celebrated in the traditional way with nativity scenes throughout the village

PUBLIC HOLIDAYS

1 Jan	New Year's Day
March/April	Easter Monday
May	Ascension Day
1 May	Labour Day
8 May	Victory in Europe Day 1945
14 July	Bastille Day
15 Aug	Assumption Day
1 Nov	All Saints' Day
11 Nov	Armistice Day 1918
19 Nov	National Holiday in Monaco
25 Dec	Christmas Day

LINKS, BLOGS, APPS & MORE

www.nicetourisme.com is the official tourism website for Nice. It has lots of listing and information including accommodation, transport links, cultural events, places of interest and webcams

www.rivieratimes.com The online English edition of The Riviera Times newspaper published for the French/Italian Riviera and the Principality of Monaco. It has news, features, listings of events and a classified section

www.frenchriviera-tourism.com The official tourism portal for the French Riviera with local booking systems, promotional deals, ge-neral information listings and an interactive map

french-riviera-blog.com Englishman Kevin Hin writes in English about his adopted home on the Côte d'Azur. Current information and tips for travellers

www.ben-vautier.com Early in the 1960, Benjamin Vautier and a number of his artist colleagues founded the Fluxus Movement in Germany with happenings and performances. Even in later life, the artist from Nice, who has his own room at the Musée d'Art Contemporain has lost none of his delight in playing with colours, shapes and letters. This site is a tasty treat for (French-speaking) art lovers who enjoy looking (and listening)

www.rebecca-marshall.com The English photographer Rebecca Marshall has the loveliest photos on the coast on her website. And tells the stories of how they came to be

www.frenchrivieratraveller.com is a blog by travel writer Jeanne Oliver who settled on the French Riviera in 1999. The site lists her sightseeing suggestions, her choice of the best beaches as well as festivals, tours and outdoor activities

Whether you are still getting ready for your trip or are already on the French Riviera, you will find more valuable information, videos and networks to add to your holiday experience at these links

VIDEOS & MUSIC

www.saint-tropez-culture.com/en Well-made videos about Saint-Tropez and its bay. As well as a 15-minute film, the site also has around 25 smaller reports

www.frenchriviera-tourism.com Lots of informative films on the coast's towns and villages on the website of the Comité Régional du Tourisme Riviera-Côte d'Azur

www.rivieraradio.mc is the website of the English Riviera Radio 106.5 with updates every hour, special features, station and local events, news, weather and links to previous shows

www.provenceweb.fr is an online magazine with cultural events and a media section that has a wide selection of videos on many of the towns and villages on the French Riviera

www.la-provence-verte.net/decouvrir/photos-provence.php Provence's official site with slideshows, some short videos and information about local markets, activities, recommended routes and more

APPS

Monaco iPhone Guide A mobile guide with a wealth of information on the Principality's attractions, local culture, nightlife, hotels and much more. It also has some great pictures and also launches Google maps to locate where you are. Download it for free from the official Monaco homepage *www.visitmonaco.com*

Saint-Tropez is an interactive magazine guide that promises to give you 'St-Tropez at your fingertips' with photo galleries, editorials, hotels, holiday rentals, history and lots of professionals listed

Nice Aéroport A free app that offers real time flight information, arrivals and departures, a flight search facility and useful telephone numbers

Sortir by Nice Matin The local paper is on the counters of every bar, and is the source of information when it comes to where to go. In summer in particular, there is an absolute abundance of festivals and concerts on the French Riviera. In French

TRAVEL TIPS

ARRIVAL

🚌 A rather long car trip so you should allow plenty of time for safe travel. A suggested route would be to make the short channel crossing and then follow the French motorway route the A26 and A7 Calais–Reims–Chaumont–Dijon–Bourg-en-Bresse–Lyon and then down to Nice. Calais–Nice is 1238 km/769 mi. Most of the motorway should be fairly clear however there are usually bottlenecks around Lyon and the Rhone valley. Toll fees or *péage* are applicable on many motorways. Avoid making Saturday your day of arrival at your destination in between mid July and mid August – traffic jams that go on for miles tend to be the order of the day.

🚆 There are a number of train travel options, one would be to take the Eurostar from London to Paris, then link to the high-speed TGV in Paris. From Paris the TGV takes less than three hours to reach Marseille, from where you can carry on by rail to Toulon, Les Arcs and Saint-Raphaël all the way to Nice. It is advisable to make an advance reservation for the TGV *(uk.voyages-sncf.com)*. Between Fréjus and Menton there is the Marseille–Toulon–Genoa rail link all the way along the coast. Hyères is connected to Toulon by a branch terminal railway line. The regional TER train runs between Grasse and Cannes directly connecting the hinterland with the French Riviera all the way to Nice.

✈️ Various national and independent airlines fly direct or via Paris to the French Riviera's main airport Nice–Côte d'Azur *(www.nice.aeroport.fr)* as well as to the other major provincial airports like Lyon and Marseille. Coaches run by *Phocéens Cars (tel. 04 93 85 62 15)* leave directly from the airport several times a day for Le Cannet, Mandelieu, Fréjus, Le Muy, Brignoles and Marseille. The first budget airlines now also fly to Toulon-Hyères airport.

RESPONSIBLE TRAVEL

It doesn't take a lot to be environmentally friendly whilst travelling. Don't just think about your carbon footprint whilst flying to and from your holiday destination but also about how you can protect nature and culture abroad. As a tourist it is especially important to respect nature, look out for local products, cycle instead of driving, save water and much more. If you would like to find out more about eco-tourism please visit: *www.ecotourism.org*

BANKS & CREDIT CARDS

Main business hours for banks: *Mon–Fri 8.30am–noon* and *2pm–5pm*. You will find ATMs in every town. Credit cards are accepted in all major hotels as well as in restaurants, shops, supermarkets, toll roads *(péage)* and petrol/gas stations.

BICYCLE HIRE

Bicycles can now be hired in Nice and it has an ever increasing network of cycle paths. One option is Vélo Bleu which has 120 bicycle stations with 1200 bicycles that can be hired using your credit card *(www.veloblue.org)*. A seven day ticket costs 5 euros which includes 30 minutes of usage per day. An additional

From arrival to weather

hour costs 1 euro. Bicycles with electric motors are hired from *Eco-Loc (Wilson car park | at the harbour | Villefranche-sur-Mer | tel. 06 66 92 72 41 | www.ecoloc06.fr)* at a relatively high rate *(7 euros for 1 hour, 30 euros for 1 day)*.

CAMPING

Regional camping guides are available from all tourist offices. The *Guide Officiel Camping Caravaning* can be obtained from *Groupe Motor Presse France (12, Rue Rouget de Lisle | Issy-les-Moulineaux | tel. 01 41 33 37 37)*. You can also view it at *www.camping france.com*.

Camp sites are increasingly attaching importance to environmentally friendly issues. With this in mind cars bare completely banned from the inner area of the ◐ *Parc et Plage (28, Rue des Langoustiers | Hyères-les-Palmiers | tel. 04 94 66 31 77 | www.parc-plage.com)*. Electric cars take guests to their camping site. The facility with all its trees, flowers and shrubs is maintained using organic products and only energy saving lamps are used.

CONSULATES & EMBASSIES

BRITISH CONSULATE
10, Place de la Joliette | Marseille | tel. 04 91 15 72 10

HONORARY BRITISH CONSUL
26, Av. Notre Dame | Nice | tel. 04 67 15 52 07

CONSULATE GENERAL
Place Varian Fry | Marseille | tel. 01 43 12 48 85

CUSTOMS

EU citizens can import and export goods for their personal use tax free (800 cigarettes, 1 kg/2.2 lbs tobacco, 90 L wine, 10 L of spirits over 22 %). Visitors from other countries must observe the following limits, except for items for personal use. Duty free are: max 50 g/0.11 lbs perfume, 200 cigarettes, 50 cigars, 250 g/0.55 lbs tabacco, 1 L spirits (over 22 % vol) and 2 L of any wine.

DRINKING WATER

Tap water is safe to drink *(eau potable)* and in restaurants the locals tend to prefer the *carafe d'eau* to expensive mineral water. In many towns and villages there are public water fountains.

DRIVING

Maximum speed limit: on the motorway 130 km/h/80 mph (if it is raining 110 km/h/68 mph); on Route National or Route Département (N, D) 90 km/h/55 mph (if it is raining 80 km/h/50 mph); in built-up areas 50 km/h/30 mph. The coastal roads are very busy in peak season and are strictly policed, cash fines can be hefty. The legal alcohol limit is 0.5. Warning triangles and yellow hi-viz vests are compulsory in cars. A device for a breathalyzer tests is recommended but, contrary to the original announcement, there is no penalty for tourists who do not have one with them.

If your car breaks down the police may be able to assist in having your vehicle towed *(dépanneur-remorqueur)* or you can call a tow company via the roadside emergency phone or by dialling 17. If you have an accident the police only need to be called if someone has been injured. Always carry your registration documents and drivers licence with you.

ELECTRICITY

France has the same 220 volt as most European countries. You will need an adapter if you want to use a UK plug.

EMERGENCY SERVICES

112 is the main emergency number as is the case in the whole of Europe

FOREST FIRE HAZARD

Safety measures to prevent forest fires are stringent in summer and areas like the *Massif de l'Esterel* and the *Massif des Maures* can be closed from July to mid September because of the winds and drought that exacerbate the fire risk. For fire warnings in the Département Var (only in summer and in French) dial *tel. 04 98 10 55 41*. For information on the areas at risk go to *www. var.gouv.fr*. Local tourist offices also issue information.

HEALTH

If you are a UK resident, before going abroad apply for a free European Health Insurance Card (EHIC) from the NHS, which should theoretically allow you access to medical treatment while travelling. It is worth noting that the new European health card is not (yet) being accepted by doctors in France as French card machines are only set for the local plastic cards. Private medical travel insurance is highly recommended.

INFORMATION

ATOUT FRANCE (FRENCH TOURIST BOARD OFFICES)
300 High Holborn | Lincoln House | London | tel. +44 20 7061 6600 | uk.france.fr
825 3rd Ave | New York | tel. 212 838 7800 | franceguide.com

COMITÉ RÉGIONAL DU TOURISME RIVIERA–CÔTE D'AZUR
455, Promenade des Anglais | 06203 Nice Cedex 03 | tel. 04 93 37 78 78 | www. cotedazur-tourisme.com

COMITÉ RÉGIONAL DU TOURISME PROVENCE-ALPES–CÔTE D'AZUR
Ne Noailles | 62-64 La Canebière | 13001 Marseille | tel. 04 91 56 47 00 | www. tourismepaca.fr

MAISON DES ALPES DE HAUTE-PROVENCE
Immeuble François Mitterrand | 8, Rue Bad Mergentheim | 04005 Digne-les-Bains | tel. 04 92 31 57 29 | www.alpes-haute-provence.com

VAR TOURISME
1, Blvd. de Strasbourg | 83000 Toulon | tel. 04 94 18 59 60 | www.visitvar.fr

INTERNET CAFÉS & WIFI

All the big towns have Internet cafés, as do the villages in the hinterland. Be aware that the names and the owners change frequently. You can also check your email and surf the Internet in cafés and libraries such as the *Bibliothèque Louis Nucéra (Tue–Sat | 2, Place Yves Klein | bmvr.nice. fr)*. in Nice.

Most hotels have Internet connections. Wi-Fi hot spots for guests with their own laptops are now part of the standard services provided by many hotels and in the yacht harbours between Hyères and Nice.

NATURISM

France has a tradition of naturism. The naturist village *Héliopolis* was founded in 1931 on the Ile du Levant, one of the "Golden Islands" off Hyères, where nudity is almost expected on all the beaches, although some clothing – what the French call *le minimum* – is required on the village square, in the harbour, and in restaurants. Although there has been a decline in the popularity of nudism in recent years, it is still expected on campsites such as *Origan Village (2160, Route du Savet | tel. 04 93 05 06 00 | www. origan-village.com)*. Further information on nudist beaches and campsites is available at *naturisme.fr* or *ffn-naturisme.com* in the Internet.

NEWSPAPERS

Biggest regional daily newspapers are *Nice Matin* and *Var Matin* with excellent events calendars. The bigger towns and cities all sell English newspapers. The local English language newspaper is *The Riviera Times (rivieratimes.com)* published for the French/Italian Riviera and the Principality of Monaco.

OPENING HOURS

Shops in the city centre are generally open from *9am–7pm Mon–Sat*, although some shop owners may take the day off on a Monday. By contrast, the large supermarkets and malls with their petrol/gas stations just outside Nice, Antibes and Toulon, even in Vence, Grasse and Fréjus are open *until 9pm Mon–Sat* some even stay open until *10pm*. In the tourist regions France has relaxed its Sunday trading ban and many shops on the French Riviera remain open the whole weekend. In the big cities bakeries, butchers and grocery stores are generally open on a Sunday morning.

PETS

UK residents can take their dog to the French Riviera on holiday using a EU Pet Passport. They need to be at least three months old, have had their anti-rabies inoculation and fitted with a microchip. It is advisable to check out the PETS (Pet Travel Scheme) website before you go for details of all requirements and for information about any re-entry conditions into your country of origin *(direct.gov. uk)*. When you book your hotel, be sure to check whether dogs are accepted as there is usually a surcharge.

CURRENCY CONVERTER

£	€	€	£
1	1.15	1	0.88
3	3.45	3	2.64
5	5.75	5	4.40
13	14.95	13	11.44
40	46	40	35.20
75	86.25	75	66
120	138	120	105.60
250	287.50	250	220
500	575	500	440

$	€	€	$
1	0.90	1	1.10
3	2.70	3	3.30
5	4.50	5	5.50
13	11.70	13	14.30
40	36	40	44
75	67.50	75	82.50
120	108	120	132
250	225	250	275
500	450	500	550

For current exchange rates see www.xe.com

PHONE & MOBILE PHONE

Most of the public phones on the French Riviera are card phones. You can buy cards from the post office or from tobacconists. The code for calling France from abroad is 0033, for Monaco 00 377. To call other countries, dial the country code (UK 0044, US 001, Ireland 00353), and then the telephone number without 0.

The French word for mobile or cell phone is *portable*. There are three main competing service providers in the area: *Cegetel (www.sfr.fr), Orange (www.orange.com | also in English)* and *Bouygues (www.bouyguestelecom.fr)*. Reception is good except in some places outside the cities.

POST

Letters and postcards in EU countries cost 1.10 euros, to the rest of the world 1.30 euros. Monaco issues its own stamps. Post offices are generally open from *9am–noon* and *2pm–5pm Mon–Fri and 9am–noon Sat.* You can also buy stamps from tobacconists, or when you purchase a postcard.

BUDGETING

Perfume	from 26 £/33 $
	for a fragrance from Grasse in a 30 ml bottle
Coffee	from 1.15 £/1.45 $
	for an espresso
Beach lounger	16.70 £/21.30 $
	per day in Nice
Wine	from 7 £/9 $
	per carafe (0.5 L)
Petrol/gas	around 1.20 £/1.50 $
	for 1 L Super
Sandwich	3.10 £/3.90 $
	for a cheese sandwich

PRIVATE ACCOMMODATION

A value for money alternative to staying in a hotel are the *chambres d'hôtes*, which offer quality accommodation in private homes and are the French equivalent of a bed and breakfast. Bookings: *Maison des Gîtes de France (59, Rue Saint-Lazare | 75009 Paris | tel. 01 49 70 75 75 | www.gites-de-france.com)*. Local tourist offices can also assist you with their own lists of *chambres d'hôtes*. Other bed and breakfast umbrella organisations for the south of France are *Fleurs de Soleil (www.fleursdesoleil.fr), Atraveo (www.atraveo.com)* and *Clévacances (www.clevacances.com)*. The *gîte rural* or holiday cottage in the countryside is also popular in France. Usually they have to be booked for a minimum of a week. France's biggest contact for vacation homes is *Pierre & Vacances (www.pierreetvacances.com)*. Another big name is *Inter-Chalet (www.interchalet.co.uk)*. For offers from private individuals go to *www.homelidays.com*

PUBLIC TRANSPORT

It can be quite difficult to get around without a car on the French Riviera, especially in the hinterland. There is an efficient public transport system (bus and train) along the coast, even though visitors may not find the timetables and ticket prices all that easy to follow. Nice has had a tramway again for a number of years, and a second line is planned to open in 2019 between the harbour and the airport.

The *Lignes d'Azur* is excellent for both local and visiting commuters alike. You pay a flat fare of 1.50 euro for any journey on the 60 or so bus routes in Département Alpes-Maritimes *(www.cg06.fr)*. There are stops in cities like Grasse, Cannes, Antibes, Menton and Nice, as well as in some of the hinterland villages.

TIPPING

Tipping *(pourboire)* is not obligatory but is normal unless the service is below par and you tip as you would back home.

WEATHER, WHEN TO GO

Peak season on the French Riviera is during the French school holidays from the beginning of July to the end of August when the region is very overcrowded. The best time to travel to the French Riviera is in late spring or autumn. Prices drop from the beginning of September (especially for accommodation) as it is the *rentrée* for the French, in other words when the French return to their everyday life. This is also the time of year when the summer is no longer as oppressively hot, but when temperatures in the Mediterranean are still suitable for swimming. Early spring is also a good time to visit the French Riviera as the locals have very few holidays around this time. The region is also magnificent in winter when the first mimosa blossoms start making their appearance in January signalling in the warmer months. In some instances, even the palatial four-star hotels in Nice, Cannes and Antibes will reduce their prices by up to 50 per cent of what they charge during season.

YOUTH HOSTELS

You will need an International Youth Hostel Pass to stay in cities like Menton, Fréjus or Cap d'Antibes. You can join before you travel or once you have arrived. For further information: *Fédération Unie des Auberges de Jeunesse | 27 Rue Pajol | 75018 Paris | tel. 01 44 89 87 27| www.fuaj.org*

WEATHER IN NICE

	Jan	Feb	March	April	May	June	July	Aug	Sept	Oct	Nov	Dec
Daytime temperatures in °C/°F	13/55	13/55	15/59	17/63	20/68	24/75	27/81	27/81	25/77	21/70	17/63	13/55
Nighttime temperatures in °C/°F	4/39	5/41	7/45	9/48	13/55	16/61	18/64	18/64	16/61	12/54	8/46	5/41
☀ Sunshine hours/day	5	6	6	8	9	10	12	11	9	7	5	5
🌂 Precipitation days/month	7	6	6	7	6	3	2	3	6	8	8	7
〰 Water temperature in °C/°F	13/55	12/54	13/55	14/57	16/61	20/68	22/72	23/73	21/70	19/66	16/61	14/57

USEFUL PHRASES FRENCH

IN BRIEF

Yes/No/Maybe	oui/non/peut-être
Please/Thank you	s'il vous plaît/merci
Good morning!/afternoon!/evening!/night!	Bonjour!/Bonjour!/Bonsoir!/Bonne nuit!
Hello!/goodbye!/See you!	Salut!/Au revoir!/Salut!
Excuse me, please	Pardon!
My name is ...	Je m'appelle ...
I'm from ...	Je suis de ...
May I ...?/ Pardon?	Puis-je ...?/Comment?
I would like to .../have you got ...?	Je voudrais .../Avez-vous?
How much is ...?	Combien coûte ...?
I (don't) like this.	Ça (ne) me plaît (pas).
good/bad/broken	bon/mauvais/cassé
too much/much/little	trop/beaucoup/peu
all/nothing	tout/rien
Help!/Attention!	Au secours/attention
police/fire brigade/ambulance	police/pompiers/ambulance
Could you please help me?	Est-ce que vous pourriez m'aider?
Do you speak English?	Parlez-vous anglais?
Do you understand?	Est-ce que vous comprenez?
Could you please ...?	Pourriez vous ... s'il vous plait?
... repeat that	répéter
... speak more slowly	parler plus lentement
... write that down	l'écrire

DATE & TIME

Monday/Tuesday	lundi/mardi
Wednesday/Thursday	mercredi/jeudi
Friday/Saturday/Sunday	vendredi/samedi/dimanche
working day/holiday	jour ouvrable/jour férié
today/tomorrow/yesterday	aujourd'hui /demain/hier
hour/minute	heure/minute
day/night/week	jour/nuit/semaine
month/year	mois/année
What time is it?	Quelle heure est-t-il?

Parlez-vous français?

"Do you speak French?" This guide will help you to say the basic words and phrases in French.

It's three o'clock.	Il est trois heures.
It's half past three.	Il est trois heures et demi.
a quarter to four	quatre heures moins le quart

TRAVEL

open/closed	ouvert/fermé
entrance/exit	entrée/sortie
departure/arrival	départ/arrivée
toilets/restrooms / ladies/gentlemen	toilettes/ femmes/hommes
(no) drinking water	eau (non) potable
Where is ...?/ Where are ...?	Où est ...?/ Où sont ...?
left/right	à gauche/à droite
straight ahead/back	tout droit/en arrière
close/far	près/loin
bus/tram/underground /taxi	bus/tramway/métro/taxi
stop/taxi stand	arrêt/station de taxi
parking lot/parking garage	parking
street map/map	plan de ville/carte routière
train station/harbour/airport	gare/port/aéroport
schedule/ticket	horaire/billet
single/return	aller simple/aller-retour
train/track/platform	train/voie/quai
I would like to rent ... a car/ a bicycle/ a boat	Je voudrais ... louer. une voiture/ un vélo/ un bateau

FOOD & DRINK

The menu, please.	La carte, s'il vous plaît.
Could I please have ...?	Puis-je avoir ... s'il vous plaît
bottle/carafe/glass	bouteille/carafe/verre
knife/fork/spoon	couteau/fourchette/cuillère
salt/pepper/sugar	sel/poivre/sucre
vinegar/oil	vinaigre/huile
milk/cream/lemon	lait/crème/citron

cold/too salty/not cooked	froid/trop salé/pas cuit
with/without ice/sparkling	avec/sans glaçons/gaz
vegetarian	végétarien(ne)
May I have the bill, please.	Je voudrais payer, s'il vous plaît
bill/receipt	addition/reçu

SHOPPING

pharmacy/chemist	pharmacie/droguerie
baker/market	boulangerie/marché
shopping centre	centre commercial
department store	grand magasin
100 grammes/1 kilo	cent grammes/un kilo
expensive/cheap/price	cher/bon marché/prix
more/less	plus/moins
organically grown	de l'agriculture biologique

ACCOMMODATION

I have booked a room	J'ai réservé une chambre
Do you have any ... left?	Avez-vous encore ...?
single room/double room	chambre simple/double
breakfast	petit déjeuner
half board/full board (American plan)	demi-pension/pension complète
shower/sit-down bath	douche/bain
balcony/terrace	balcon /terrasse
key/room card	clé/carte magnétique
luggage/suitcase/bag	bagages/valise/sac

BANKS, MONEY & CREDIT CARDS

bank/ATM/pin code	banque/guichet automatique/code
cash/credit card	comptant/carte de crédit
bill/coin	billet/monnaie

HEALTH

doctor/dentist/paediatrician	médecin/dentiste/pédiatre
hospital/emergency clinic	hôpital/urgences
fever/pain	fièvre/douleurs
diarrhoea/nausea	diarrhée/nausée
sunburn	coup de soleil
inflamed/injured	enflammé/blessé
plaster/bandage	pansement/bandage
ointment/pain reliever	pommade/analgésique

POST, TELECOMMUNICATIONS & MEDIA

stamp	timbre
lettre/postcard	lettre/carte postale
I need a landline phone card.	J'ai besoin d'une carte téléphonique pour fixe.
I'm looking for a prepaid card for my mobile.	Je cherche une recharge pour mon portable.
Where can I find internet access?	Où puis-je trouver un accès à internet?
dial/connection/engaged	composer/connection/occupé
socket/charger	prise électrique/chargeur
computer/battery/ rechargeable battery	ordinateur/batterie/ accumulateur
at sign (@)	arobase
internet address (URL)/e-mail address	adresse internet/mail
internet connection/wifi	accès internet/wi-fi
e-mail/file/print	mail/fichier/imprimer

LEISURE, SPORTS & BEACH

beach	plage
sunshade/lounger	parasol/transat
low tide/high tide/current	marée basse/marée haute/courant
cable car/chair lift	téléphérique/télésiège
(rescue) hut	refuge

NUMBERS

0	zéro	17	dix-sept
1	un, une	18	dix-huit
2	deux	19	dix-neuf
3	trois	20	vingt
4	quatre	30	trente
5	cinq	40	quarante
6	six	50	cinquante
7	sept	60	soixante
8	huit	70	soixante-dix
9	neuf	80	quatre-vingt
10	dix	90	quatre-vingt-dix
11	onze	100	cent
12	douze	200	deux cents
13	treize	1000	mille
14	quatorze		
15	quinze	½	un[e] demi[e]
16	seize	¼	un quart

ROAD ATLAS

The green line indicates the Discovery Tour „French Riviera at a glance"
The blue line indicates the other Discovery Tours

All tours are also marked on the pull-out map

Photo: The bay of Agay at the Corniche de l'Esterel

Exploring the French Riviera

The map on the back cover shows how
the area has been sub-divided

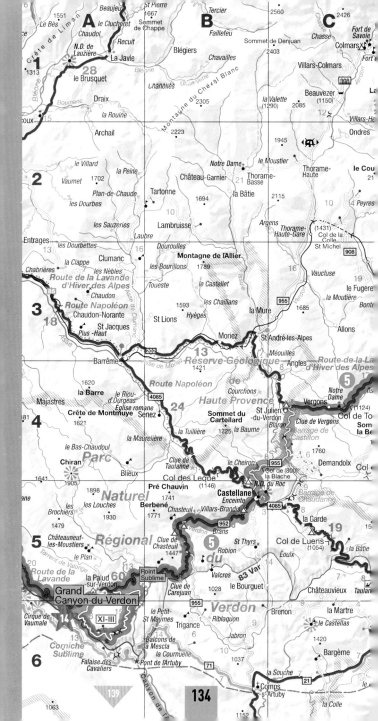

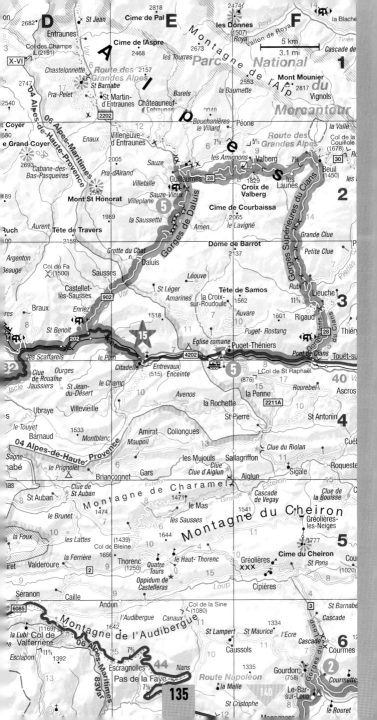

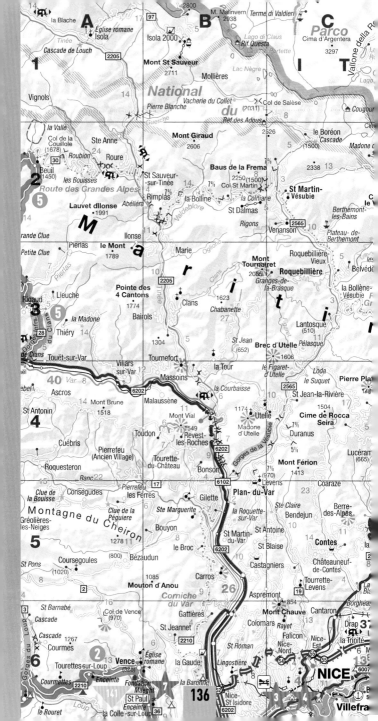

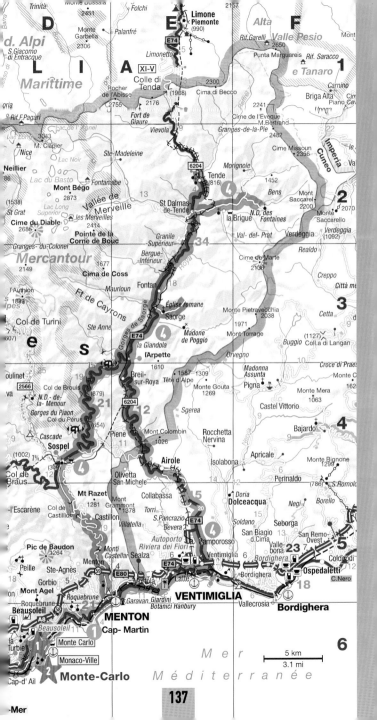

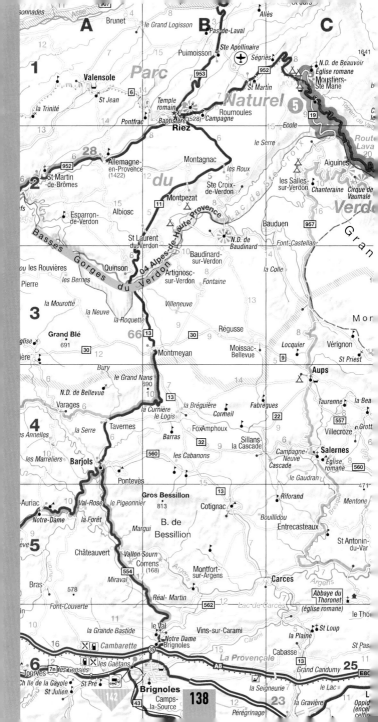

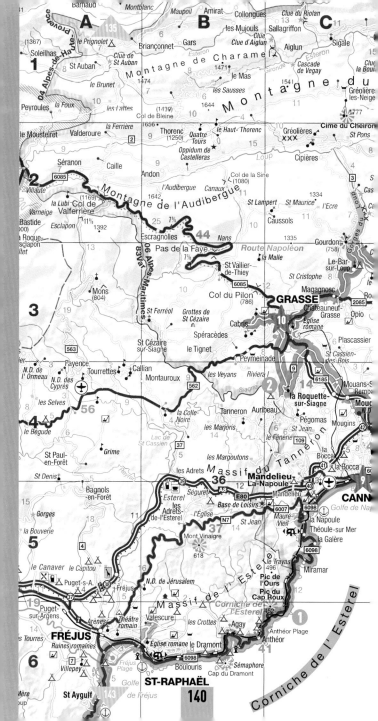

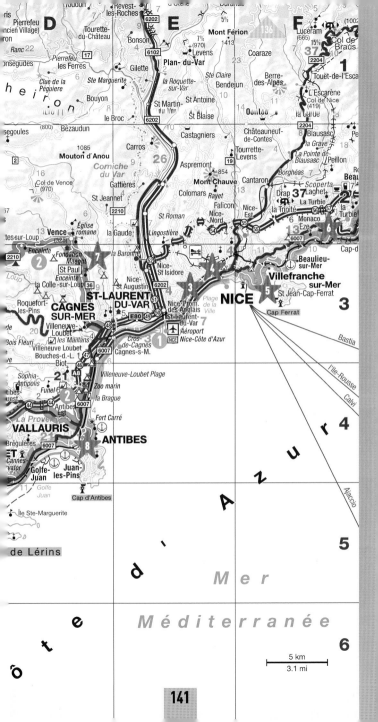

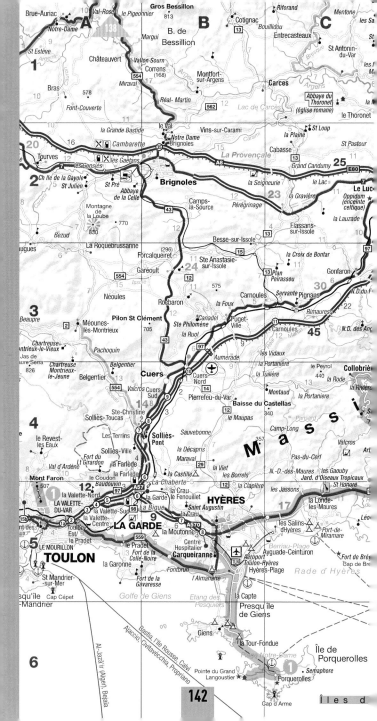

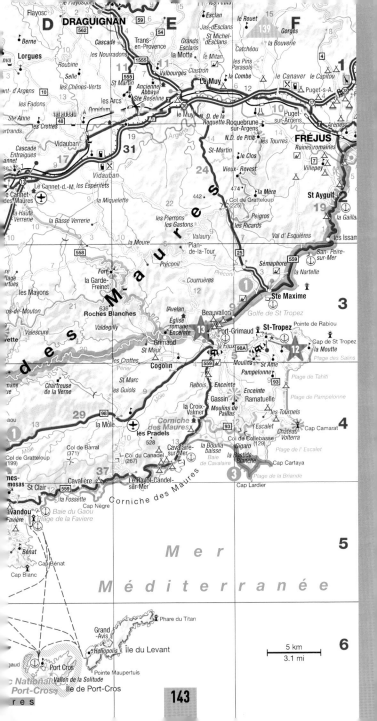

KEY TO ROAD ATLAS

German	Symbol	English
Autobahn mit Anschlussstelle und Anschlussnummern	Viernheim	Motorway with junction and junction number
Autobahn in Bau mit voraussichtlichem Fertigstellungsdatum	Datum / Date	Motorway under construction with expected date of opening
Rasthaus mit Übernachtung · Raststätte	Kassel ✕	Hotel, motel · Restaurant
Kiosk · Tankstelle		Snackbar · Filling-station
Autohof · Parkplatz mit WC	P	Truckstop · Parking place with WC
Autobahn-Gebührenstelle		Toll station
Autobahnähnliche Schnellstraße		Dual carriageway with motorway characteristics
Fernverkehrsstraße		Trunk road
Verbindungsstraße		Main road
Nebenstraßen		Secondary roads
Fahrweg · Fußweg		Carriageway · Footpath
Gebührenpflichtige Straße		Toll road
Straße für Kraftfahrzeuge gesperrt	X X X X X	Road closed for motor vehicles
Straße für Wohnanhänger gesperrt		Road closed for caravans
Straße für Wohnanhänger nicht empfehlenswert		Road not recommended for caravans
Autofähre · Autozug-Terminal		Car ferry · Autorail station
Hauptbahn · Bahnhof · Tunnel		Main line railway · Station · Tunnel
Besonders sehenswertes kulturelles Objekt	♪ Neuschwanstein	Cultural site of particular interest
Besonders sehenswertes landschaftliches Objekt	✳ Breitachklamm	Landscape of particular interest
MARCO POLO Erlebnistour 1		MARCO POLO Discovery Tour 1
MARCO POLO Erlebnistouren		MARCO POLO Discovery Tours
MARCO POLO Highlight	⭐1	MARCO POLO Highlight
Landschaftlich schöne Strecke		Route with beautiful scenery
Touristenstraße	Hanse-Route	Tourist route
Museumseisenbahn		Tourist train
Kirche, Kapelle · Kirchenruine Kloster · Klosterruine	✝	Church, chapel · Church ruin Monastery · Monastery ruin
Schloss, Burg · Burgruine Turm · Funk-, Fernsehturm		Palace, castle · Castle ruin Tower · Radio or TV tower
Leuchtturm · Windmühle Denkmal · Soldatenfriedhof		Lighthouse · Windmill Monument · Military cemetery
Ruine, frühgeschichtliche Stätte · Höhle Hotel, Gasthaus, Berghütte · Heilbad		Archaeological excavation, ruins · Cave Hotel, inn, refuge · Spa
Campingplatz · Jugendherberge Schwimmbad, Erlebnisbad, Strandbad · Golfplatz	△ ⛺ △	Camping site · Youth hostel Swimming pool, leisure pool, beach · Golf-course
Botanischer Garten, sehenswerter Park · Zoologischer Garten		Botanical gardens, interesting park · Zoological garden
Bedeutendes Bauwerk · Bedeutendes Areal	▪ ◻	Important building · Important area
Verkehrsflughafen · Regionalflughafen	✈ ⊕	Airport · Regional airport
Flugplatz · Segelflugplatz	⊕	Airfield · Gliding site
Boots- und Jachthafen	⚓	Marina

INDEX

This index lists all places, sights and beaches featured in this guide. Numbers in bold indicate a main entry